Stand Up And Be Counted

Also by R. T. Kendall

JONAH
TITHING
WHO BY FAITH
ONCE SAVED, ALWAYS SAVED
CALVIN AND ENGLISH CALVINISM
   TO 1649

Stand Up And Be Counted

by

R. T. Kendall

HODDER AND STOUGHTON
LONDON SYDNEY AUCKLAND TORONTO

Biblical quotations are taken from the Authorised Version unless otherwise indicated

British Library Cataloguing in Publication Data

Kendall, R.T.
   Stand up and be counted.—
   (Hodder Christian paperbacks)
   1. Evangelistic work
   I. Title
   269'.2   BV3790

ISBN 0 340 35175 6

Hodder and Stoughton Editorial Office: 47 Bedford Square, London WC1B 3DP.

To every Evangelist

Contents

Foreword

By its very nature, the gospel of Jesus Christ demands decision on the part of its hearers. In this significant book, the Rev R.T. Kendall has given us an incisive and biblical analysis of the importance of calling people to take a public stand for Christ – not just during special evangelistic missions, but as a regular practice within the local church. He speaks from his deep knowledge of both the Bible and Church history, as well as from his wide experience as a pastor. His insights could revolutionise and revitalise countless churches.

Billy Graham

Preface

I am indebted to Dr Robert L. Asa, recent graduate of Southern Baptist Theological Seminary of Louisville, Kentucky. Dr Asa provided me with valuable source material when he was a doctoral student of Dr Lewis Drummond, the Billy Graham Professor of Evangelism there. This information was especially relevant to the 'roots and shoots' of chapter two. Readers may also want to consult Dr Drummond's own book *Charles Grandison Finney* (Hodders, 1983).

It is not possible to mention all who have had a hand in the making of this little book. But a number of scholars have been most co-operative when I turned to them with questions: Dr Geoffrey F. Nuttall, Dr John Kent, Dr A. Skevington Wood, the Rev Herbert McGonigle, Dr B.R. White, Dr Eric Hayden and Dr Phil Roberts.

Miss Carolyn Armitage of Hodder and Stoughton has been extremely helpful and encouraging. Mr Richard Alderson, as always, has read the manuscript and has been of immense help. My greatest debt, however, is to my wife, who reads everything I write before anyone else sees it, and has given wonderful counsel along the way.

One of the highlights of my life was on May 6th of this year when I introduced Dr Billy Graham to a Sunday evening congregation at Westminster Chapel. He left his hospital bed to preach for us, and it was truly a night of nights. Dr Graham has also kindly read what follows and I do thank him for his encouragement. I warmly dedicate this book to every evangelist, and I should like to think that every servant of the Lord will feel that this therefore includes himself.

R.T. Kendall
London, July 1984

Introduction

On 15th April 1982, moments before I introduced him to a special gathering of over 2,500 people in Westminster Chapel, Arthur Blessitt made a passing comment to me about the 'invitation' he would give at the close of his address. I looked at him and said abruptly, 'You're not going to do that, are you? That's not done here.' He was calm. I pulled myself together and said, 'Well, if you feel led, go ahead.' His reply was, 'I can tell you right now, I do.' He did, and Westminster Chapel has never been the same since.

After the 1983 phase of 'Mission to London' was completed, Dr Luis Palau was asked what he had learned from British Christians and what he felt they had yet to learn. On the former point, Dr Palau stressed three things to his interviewer. 'First, you are gifted in organisation; second, you know about discipling new converts; third, you take words very seriously – if someone says something, you listen!' He continued: 'When you ask what you have to learn, please remember I'm generalising. But – one, the Church must return to the authority of the Bible, read the Bible, preach the Bible without defending it or apologising for it. Two, we should call for decisions regularly in our churches, perhaps once a month, without waiting for a special mission. Three, learn the value of consecutive expository preaching – the churches doing this are the big ones numerically.'

This book takes up Luis Palau's point about calling for decisions regularly without waiting for a 'Mission to London' or 'Mission England'. This book directly addresses the issue whether the practice of calling people 'forward' or 'to the front' at the close of the evangelistic sermon is suitable for churches in their regular services. It is expected that Dr Billy Graham is going to do this when he preaches in an evangelistic service. But should the vicar or minister of a local congregation do this? Should this practice not be left to men like Billy Graham, Luis Palau or Arthur Blessitt? Or is there a case to be made that such a practice should be brought right into the Church itself?

I write this book to support this practice – which I prefer to call 'public pledge', a phrase I shall define below. I know of books and articles which have opposed this practice. But I write to urge its use in every church. It is a practice that can be abused, and I shall look at ways in which this has happened. But I have come to the conclusion that our calling men to come out of hiding and stand up and be counted is right, relevant and theologically sound. Most of all, it is honouring to God.

I shall be thankful to my dying day that Arthur Blessitt did not take his cue from me on that memorable night. What gripped me most on that evening was not merely the number of people who came forward to confess Christ but the liberty and power with which Arthur spoke.

A few days later I asked Arthur if he would consider remaining in London for the next few weeks and preach in Westminster Chapel on the Sunday nights. His reply was, 'If I did agree to stay, are you going to handcuff me or let me be myself?' I assured him that I had already sorted that one out – he must be himself without any strings attached. He agreed to stay and preached for us on six consecutive Sunday nights, closing at the end of May 1982. There is no way at the present time to calculate the effect those six weeks had on Westminster Chapel in general and myself in particular. In addition to the 'innovations' he brought into the services, he got us out on the streets talking to people about Jesus Christ. The 'invitation' he gave at each service was in a sense a very small part of the contribution he made to us.

My problem was what to do after he left! One of the most difficult times of my life was that first week in June. I agonised during the entire week. What should I do? Should I continue with what Arthur had started, or should we go back to 'business as usual'? I finally concluded that Arthur's time with us would be largely wasted if we returned to our normal routine. Not all felt as I did about Arthur and I knew that to continue with what Arthur began would alienate some of those who had supported my ministry. But in my heart of hearts I knew that God sent Arthur to give Westminster Chapel a good shaking up and that I would quench the Spirit to sweep what He had done under the carpet.

On the first Saturday after Arthur left, six people joined me to talk to people in the streets in the area of Buckingham Gate and Victoria about Jesus Christ. The Pilot Lights were born. On the first Sunday night in June 1982, with fear and trembling, I invited people to make a public pledge to Jesus Christ. To my surprise and delight seven people walked forward to confess Christ publicly.

I now invite people to confess Christ publicly at the close of every Sunday evening service in Westminster Chapel. There have been many times when nobody at all responded. There have been times when the only one who came forward was either an over-conscientious person or one who thought that coming forward would be a 'quick cure'. There have been times when I have actually been embarrassed and returned to the vestry with a heavy heart asking, 'Dear Lord, what have I done?' But there have been glorious nights when the sudden conversion has taken place, nights when people yielded to coming forward despite their enormous fears within, and nights when God put His undoubted seal on the service. Speaking personally, I have had more liberty in my preaching than I have ever known in my life.

But this is no 'success story'. Not at all. Neither has true revival come to Westminster Chapel. I used to think that if ever the Spirit of God came down on my preaching with extraordinary power I just might call people forward to confess Christ openly. This would have been the way of least controversy. By and large what I have done has been very scary indeed. But I have been convinced above all else that it is a God-honouring thing to do. This is what gives me peace. Not the success.

I come now to the use of terms. There is one term that I wish to refer to, then lay to rest – 'altar call'. I am not exactly sure when the term originated but it seems clear how it developed. It is sometimes thought that the practice began with the American evangelist Charles G. Finney, whose ministry extended from 1824 to 1875. This is not quite true. What is closer to the facts is that Finney popularised and systematised a practice that had its roots in the preceding century when the Great Awakening in New England was at its peak.

The latter part of the eighteenth century saw the spread of Methodism in America. In 1799 the idea of 'camp meetings' emerged and it became a phenomenon which crossed denominational lines and spread eventually all over America. It could have been any preacher who said it first, but the emphasis upon coming to God's 'mercy seat' to receive forgiveness of sins became a common way of urging the sinner to seek salvation. The term 'mercy seat' is only used once in the New Testament (AV), a translation of the Greek *hilasterion* ('place of atonement' – NIV) which is used also in Romans 3:25 ('propitiation', AV; 'sacrifice of atonement', NIV). Moses was given instructions for the building of the tabernacle in the wilderness. This architectural plan was a 'pattern' that foreshadowed its fulfilment in the death and priestly work of Jesus Christ (Exod. 25:40, Heb. 10:1). In the ancient tabernacle the place of the animal sacrifice (the altar) and the Most Holy Place were separated by a curtain. In the Most Holy Place was the ark of the covenant, an oblong chest. On the top of the chest was a slab of pure gold – the mercy seat. Once a year, on the Day of Atonement, the high priest would take some of the blood from the animal just sacrificed, go behind the curtain and sprinkle blood on the mercy seat. It was then – and only then – that the atonement for sin became effectual. When Jesus said, 'It is finished' (John 19:30 – Gr. *tetelestai*, or 'paid in full'), the veil of the temple was ripped from top to bottom (Matt. 27:51). The mercy seat on earth was abolished; the one that matters is in heaven. Thus preachers would invite people to come and cast themselves on God's mercy seat.

In camp meetings, and eventually in church buildings, a railing suitable for kneeling at was placed immediately in front of the pulpit. This railing, or bench, became known as the 'altar'. Thus the invitation for people to come to God's mercy seat was brought home in terms of the opportunity for people to seek the Lord by kneeling at the altar. The call for people to come forward hence became known as the 'altar call'. This to me has a lovely origin.

However, the term altar call is confusing to most people today, especially if they have a Catholic background. To Catholics the altar is the place of the Eucharist, often in an ornate setting, presided over by the priest. The term might be even more puzzling to the Jew.

And yet another reason for leaving the term altar call to one side is that not all who come forward – even if they kneel – truly reach God's mercy seat. The danger is that one may get the impression that just because he walks to the front something must happen to him. In other words, not all who come forward get to God. Although never intended, the altar call – even by any other name – can be idolatrous.

Before the arrival of Billy Graham in Britain years ago the practice of calling people forward was called 'making an appeal'. Dr Graham called it 'giving the invitation'. But such terms can and no doubt should be the thrust and content of the evangelistic sermon itself. Surely a good evangelistic sermon has the invitation to receive Christ all the way through!

I prefer the term (or phrase) 'public pledge'. One reason for laying the other terms to one side is simply that I want to make as clear as possible precisely what it is I am affirming. Public pledge comes the closest to describing the practice I feel is valid and the theology that lies behind that practice. So many things come to mind with the other terms. I have therefore chosen one that is not as yet associated with abuses.

But public pledge also needs careful examination. No doubt it too can be abused and is by no means invulnerable to idolatry and confusion. A pledge is simply the earnest token of one's sincerity or truthfulness. A pledge may of course be offered secretly between two persons. But should the pledge be made public, the one making it has put himself on the line before everybody. It is no secret, nothing is hidden.

'Pledge' was a favourite word of John Calvin in connection with his doctrine of assurance of salvation. But Calvin used the word from God's point of view, namely that Christ is presented to us as God's pledge of eternal life. Calvin even said that Christ was the pledge, or 'mirror', of our election. We simply see Jesus Christ and infer our own election to salvation. The bread and wine in the sacraments, according to Calvin, are likewise God's 'pledge and assurance of spiritual life'. God put Himself on the line in the person and work of His Son, and God's integrity is mirrored in the sacraments.

A pledge, then, is always a solemn promise. When a person 'goes public' with his faith in Jesus Christ, it is a pledge before God, the world and the devil that he believes that Jesus Christ is Lord and that God raised Him from the dead. The pledge means there is 'no turning back'. The public pledge sends a clear signal to the world that one is unashamed of Jesus. The public pledge is the open confession of a hidden work, namely the secret work of the Holy Spirit. In other words, it is the public testimony of what is in the heart. 'If you confess with your mouth, "Jesus is Lord", and believe in your heart that God raised him from the dead, you will be saved. For it is with your heart that you believe and are justified, and it is with your mouth that you confess and are saved' (Rom. 10:9–10, NIV).

Another advantage with this term is that it suggests that more is to follow. For example, in business affairs one's pledge is the surety that more (money, property, etc.) will follow in due course. When one 'goes public' by walking out to the front of the church to confess Jesus Christ as Lord and Saviour, it is not the end but the beginning. Implied therefore is the pledge to live a life under the sovereign rule of King Jesus from that day forward.

I will show below that the public pledge may also be the earnest of one's baptism – *not replacing it* but indicating one's willingness to be baptised, especially when it is not always physically possible to be baptised immediately (as was so often done in the New Testament). Thus the public pledge *temporarily* takes the place of baptism in some cases. This is of course assuming that one does not believe in baptismal regeneration (the belief that baptism itself causes one to be born again), a teaching I do not agree with.

I therefore use the term public pledge as the best way of describing the practice which I endorse, and also because it is consistent with the theology that lies behind that practice.

I come now to theology. It may surprise the reader to learn that I am a Calvinist – a real one!* By that I mean that I don't merely believe in 'once saved, always saved' but also in the doctrine of election. In my book *Once Saved, Always Saved* I explain to the reader how I came to believe in that doctrine – the knowledge that I can never be finally lost in hell. What I didn't go into in that book is what else I learned after 31st October 1955. But I should tell the reader that, despite never having heard the first preacher in my life (that I know of) who believed in such a teaching, I discovered the doctrine of election for myself in the Bible. At the time I was a student at Trevecca Nazarene College in Nashville, Tennessee, and the assistant to the Dean of Religion. I said to him one day, 'The Bible teaches that God has chosen some but not all to salvation.' With a look of shock he said to me, 'You're going off into Calvinism.' I asked, 'What is that?' 'Well,' he replied, 'it is certainly

*See appendix I for an elaboration on terms such as Calvinism and Arminianism.

something we *don't* believe.' I said, 'Then *we* are wrong.'

My point is this. I write this book as a convinced Calvinist. I say that for a number of reasons. First, I think the preponderance of literature against the invitation has been written by Calvinists. I believe there is a need to show that a Calvinist too can believe in calling for an immediate declaration of conversion and inviting people to stand up and be counted! Second, this book just might be a means of demonstrating to our Arminian friends (who believe that election is determined by faith rather than God's sovereign choice) that one does *not* have to surrender his evangelistic zeal should he become a Calvinist. I don't mean to be unfair, but I sometimes wonder if too many Calvinists (speaking generally) have done more to put people off the doctrines of sovereign grace than any intelligent attack upon it. Some Calvinists have done it largely by giving the impression (though they did not mean to do this) that they do not really care about the souls of the lost. Third, I express the hope that this book might encourage some Calvinist ministers to present the opportunity of a public pledge to their listeners. I fear that some are not going to be very anxious to charge into their pulpits on the first Sunday evening after reading this to do what is called for in this book! But I hope I will be forgiven none the less for wishing this!

I might add that I myself almost always gave a public invitation at the close of my sermon before I became the minister of my present church. When I accepted preaching opportunities in British churches, I did not give an invitation as I knew it was not usually the custom and I had no desire to become controversial over this issue. I did not regard this matter as paramount and, the truth is, I didn't think a lot about it. Thus when I was invited to preach at Westminster Chapel, it never entered my mind to give what they would call an 'appeal' – something that many tended to regard as an American innovation. After I was called to be their minister, I felt it was God's will that I should accept. I also assumed it would be my duty to be 'all things to all men' and not stir up trouble over what had not been generally done in their past. I must admit that I began to think about it a bit because I brought up the subject with one with whom I was very close. He recalled the way in which I gave an invitation in my previous church, a Southern Baptist church near Oxford, which he had visited on a number of occasions. 'I have no difficulty with that at all,' he said to me, but he did not advise me to do the same in Westminster. So I put that concern in abeyance.

I remember one evening in Westminster Chapel when I seemed to have a good deal of liberty. It was a sermon on the final judgment. A fairly prominent American minister was in the congregation (he is now in heaven). He said to me after the service that he could not understand my not giving the people an opportunity to respond to my message. He thought it was unthinkable that I should preach a sermon like that and then dismiss the crowd. I explained to him that if there was indeed conviction upon the hearts of the people, it would not go away but that I might have allowed people to come forward who were affected by emotion rather than the Holy Spirit. He disagreed and suggested I was being too controlled by my Calvinistic theology. His suggestion gave me pause.

An event that troubled me even more was a statement Joseph Ton made to me about four years ago. I did not know that Joseph was even in Britain but he was listening to my sermon one Sunday evening while standing in the vestibule of Westminster Chapel – making sure I would not detect his presence. Joseph Ton, now living in America, was then the pastor of a church in Oradea, Romania. Joseph took a degree in theology at Oxford in the late 1960s and was a member of the Westminster Chapel fraternal of ministers during that time. He understood the theological milieu of the Chapel and those who had long been associated with it. I became acquainted with him in the late 1970s and got to know him well. He surprised me when he came to the vestry that Sunday evening and revealed he had heard every word of my sermon. But he was disappointed, and this was the first time he had heard me preach. I already knew that he claimed to be helped by my book entitled *Jonah* and I was a bit hurt that he was let down when he actually heard me preach. He remarked that I did not invite people to confess Christ publicly.

'Why don't you call people forward?' he asked.

'Joseph, you know this church. I just can't do it here.'

'R. T., I too am reformed in my theology and I also understand the British. You must not be afraid to call people forward. I always did it in Oradea.'

'But this is not Oradea,' I said.

The next day the telephone rang. Joseph was phoning me from Heathrow Airport just before he left London. His word to me was this: 'You will not have liberty in Westminster Chapel until you begin calling people forward.' I thought his view was a bit strong and exaggerated. But I remembered his words when Arthur Blessitt made it clear he was going to do what he did on the night of 15th April 1982. By then I was beginning to think that God was truly dealing with me along this very line despite my own rationale for having adopted the course I had taken.

It was the conversation with Joseph Ton that first made me seriously consider the possibility of one day calling for people to come forward after a sermon in Westminster Chapel. But I wanted the *undoubted* power first – recognisable to all. Joseph's statement, or prophecy (if I dare call it that), was that I would not have freedom 'until' I began doing this. What I wanted was the freedom first, *then* I might well get away with doing such a thing in the Chapel. 'If only the Holy Spirit will come down on the Chapel in such a way that everyone can see how powerfully God is present, then I will call for people to stand up and be counted.' That was my thinking.

To put it another way, I was quite willing to be faithful in that which is 'much'. I was haunted by those words of our Lord: 'He that is faithful in that which is least is faithful also in much' (Luke 16:10). I did not particularly care to be faithful in that which was 'least' – calling for people to come forward when I *lacked* the unction I longed for. I recall the story of a missionary in Africa who preached there for twenty years without much success – but who none the less was always inviting his hearers to come forward. He found himself one day in a place where genuine revival broke out. To his amazement he witnessed people walking forward under great conviction even while he was preaching! What he had failed to get people to do for twenty years was now happening spontaneously! It would be easy to criticise the method of this missionary for twenty years – he must have felt like a fool – when the undoubted outpouring of the Spirit results in more conversions in a day than in years and years of hard work which God did not appear to own. This account in Africa can be used to refute the need to call for people to give an immediate declaration of conversion or of inviting them to stand up and be counted. It is so easy to say, 'If something is of God, it will be spontaneous.' The spontaneous can also be called the 'much'. But if the 'much' is of God, so is the 'least' – which God does not always *appear* to own, at least at first.

I would say at this moment that these are 'non-revival times'. Some may disagree. But surely all would agree that there is a great need for the kind of outpouring from heaven for which there is no natural explanation. So much that is observable today in the name of Christianity can be explained at the natural level. This would include my call for inviting men to pledge publicly their allegiance to Jesus Christ. I do not claim that doing such is always obviously the work of the Holy Spirit, much less that it will lead to authentic revival. But I want to make a case for presenting the opportunity for men and women to respond to the gospel in a manner that calls them to stand up and be counted – before everybody. It may be that God is testing us in times like these to see whether we will be faithful in that which is not so spontaneous. Whether or not something works is not always the proper test.

1

A HIGH PRIVILEGE

It is sometimes said that Billy Graham gives the Church the opportunity to do what it should be doing all the time. Surely every Church is called to be an evangelistic Church – not merely evangelical but evangelistic. If evangelical partly describes the Church's doctrinal stance, evangelistic describes in part what should be its thrust. The Church that will make an impact on the world will be the one that is seeking to save it.

It might also be stated that if the Church were doing what it ought to be doing, there would be no need for a Billy Graham crusade. What is also true is that the impact of 'mass evangelism' crusades on a particular area – be it England in general or London in particular – is often relatively minimal. The percentage of the population that is reached for Christ (even if all who professed faith are truly converted) is exceedingly small. While this might be used to dismiss altogether the validity of a Billy Graham campaign, I would argue that the Church might learn something from such and consider seriously incorporating the same evangelistic thrust and excitement into its regular services.

A young minister came to the great C. H. Spurgeon with a deep concern. The young minister thought himself sufficiently adequate in the pulpit but said, 'I don't seem to have many converts.' 'Surely you don't look for a convert every time you preach,' replied Mr Spurgeon. 'Oh no, of course not,' the young minister answered. 'That is why you are not having them,' Mr Spurgeon retorted.

Presenting the opportunity of making a public pledge reinforces the need for a person to consider the state of his own soul. It will increase the expectancy of the congregation and it will force the minister to look for a conversion before his very eyes. The call for men to commit themselves publicly to Jesus Christ will serve to bring both the minister and the congregation to the brink of expectancy for conversions in a way nothing else is likely to do – save spontaneous revival itself.

As I was preparing to write this very chapter, a minister telephoned me to state that the only thing lacking in his ministry is ,that he seems so unable to bring men to conversion. 'I realise that only the Holy Spirit can do it,' he said. 'I only wish I could somehow bring people to close with Christ.' I believe that this particular minister is being too controlled by his Calvinistic theology. To me it is almost amusing how God has used the Arminian evangelists in the world to save His elect. Too many Christians today, rather than build their church by conversions, at best seem only to hope to find another Christian (converted elsewhere) who can be 'converted' to a certain kind of teaching. Growing by conversions is a concept quite foreign to some.

It is not a very healthy church that has been sustained largely by Christians converted elsewhere. When a congregation is built up by people leaving a former congregation, the world remains the same. For the Kingdom of God is not enlarged the slightest bit. There is only one answer: fresh conversions to the Lord Jesus Christ. This is the way a church ought to grow.

I believe that presenting the opportunity of the public pledge to the non-Christian is *one* way of bringing people to conversion. It is not the only way (of course). But it is a way.

The call for a public pledge ought to be a part of the sermon, not a P.S. at the end of it. The public pledge is of course emphasised at the end, but an evangelistic sermon ought to seek to bring people to a personal commitment right from its beginning. When the non-Christian knows that he is being asked to commit his life to Christ before he leaves the premises of the church – and do so publicly – the pressure of the Holy Spirit will be on him from the start. It will not be human pressure. It is the pressure of the Spirit. For that person will be made to realise that he himself is having to face up to the claims of Jesus Christ. This brings the message home. He knows he is being called to stand up and be counted. But if there is no indication that he may have to put himself on the line, he will not be too worried over leaving the church as he came in.

'Come out of hiding' is a phrase I often use. I have seen the Holy Spirit remarkably at work in this way – from leading people to reveal who they really were to bringing people to marriage! One man who had been living falsely under an assumed name came to the Lord and admitted who he really was. A couple who had been living together for years were led to get their lives sorted out and got married. But the main thing is that the non-Christian should be told that he must *come out of hiding* if he is going to be identified with Jesus Christ. He must do so openly.

Jesus said, 'Whoever acknowledges me before men, I will also acknowledge him before my Father in heaven. But whoever disowns me before men, I will disown him before my Father in heaven' (Matt. 10:32-3, NIV). This is a very strong statement. It is sobering. If I had only one verse in the Bible to support the call for people to pledge themselves publicly to Christ, it would be this one. Not that one must walk forward in a public service in order to honour that scripture (for it equally refers to the whole of the Christian life). But pledging publicly one's commitment to Jesus Christ most certainly *does* honour it. It is a way of coming out of hiding.

All men and women will come out of hiding sooner or later. For Jesus also said, 'There is nothing concealed that will not be disclosed, or hidden that will not be made known' (Matt. 10:26, NIV). 'For there is nothing hidden that will not be disclosed, and nothing concealed that will not be known or brought out into the open' (Luke 8:17,

NIV). In other words, it is only a matter of time before everybody will learn the truth of our secrets. When the Lord comes, He 'will bring to light what is hidden in darkness and will expose the motives of men's hearts' (I Cor. 4:5, NIV). But to the one who confesses that Jesus Christ is Lord, provided that he believes in his heart that God has raised Jesus from the dead, there is the promise of *salvation* (Rom. 10:9). Salvation assures us that our sins will not be held against us. 'I will forgive their wickedness and will remember their sins no more' (Heb. 8:12, NIV). In a word: to come out of hiding now provides assurance that we will not be condemned at the final judgment.

At the final judgment everybody will confess Jesus as Lord – publicly. Openly. '"As surely as I live," says the Lord, "Every knee will bow before me; every tongue will confess to God"' (Rom. 14:11, NIV). The Apostle Paul then drew a conclusion: 'So, then, each of us will give an account of himself to God' (Rom. 14:12, NIV). I should think that to confess Jesus Christ openly before men in a public meeting now will be as *nothing* compared to the awesomeness of doing it on that last day. The public pledge allows people to prove to themselves that they are not ashamed of Jesus Christ. It will not be the last time. It is the beginning. But a wonderful beginning it is. 'If anyone is ashamed of me and my words in this adulterous and sinful generation, the Son of Man will be ashamed of him when he comes in his Father's glory with the holy angels' (Mark 8:38, NIV). The public pledge of one's faith and intentions is a demonstration that one is not ashamed of the Lord Jesus Christ.

It is only a matter of time, then, before all people will confess who Jesus is. 'At the name of Jesus every knee should bow, in heaven and on earth and under the earth, and every tongue confess that Jesus Christ is Lord, to the glory of God the Father' (Phil. 2:10–11, NIV). The day will come when all will be agreed. It is sometimes said that the Christian is 'behind the times'. Not so. The Christian is *ahead* of the times. The Christian confesses now what the whole world will confess later. The Christian does it publicly now - in terms of a pledge. The world will do it publicly later - in terms of unconditional surrender. The one who refuses to confess Christ now may win the battle, but God will win the war. 'Look, he is coming with the clouds, and every eye will see him, even those who pierced him; and all the peoples of the earth will mourn because of him. So shall it be! Amen' (Rev. 1:7, NIV).

The public pledge is in fact God's pledge to us! The invitation to stand up and be counted is God's way of saying, 'I want you - now.' The *opportunity* of confessing Jesus now signifies that it is still a day of mercy. One should be thankful that the very invitation to confess Christ is given. It is in fact God's pledge to us that 'if you confess with your mouth, "Jesus is Lord," and believe in your heart that God raised him from the dead, you will be saved' (Rom. 10:9, NIV). The public pledge, then, is really God's promise to us. 'Everyone who trusts in him will never be put to shame' (Rom. 10:11, NIV).

The presentation of the public pledge, therefore, is a kind of visual demonstration that God wants men to come to Him. It allows men and women to see for themselves just what it is they might do next in order to take God's invitation seriously. The opportunity for men to confess Christ now sends a signal from heaven that 'God accepts you *now* - as you are'. It also enables people with limited knowledge to feel that there is something they *can* do to demonstrate the earnestness of their hearts. I fear that one of the greatest mistakes many of us have made is in requiring that people have more knowledge and under-standing of the gospel than God requires in order to be saved. Many times people will feel a great surge of warmth towards the message they have just heard but lose it partly because there was no opportunity for them to 'strike while the iron is hot'. It is sometimes countered by Calvinists, 'But if it is really the Holy Spirit dealing with them, that feeling will not go away.' I wonder. I also wonder if we have a right to 'play God' like that and judge just how deeply the Spirit may be at work.

A man recently came into my vestry after a service and

told me this story. Having been brought up in a 'pagan' home, he went to a church service in Bradford for the first time in his life at the age of eighteen. A Salvation Army Officer preached the sermon. 'I have no recollection of his message,' this man said to me, but the pastor of that church, the Rev. A. Barry Blake-Lobb (at present working with the Pocket Testament League), concluded the meeting by stating that there was someone in the congregation whose life needed to be changed and that Christ could do that for him. An opportunity for a public response was made. 'I responded,' this man continued, 'knowing that my life needed changing. I do not think that at that point I understood the gospel.' The pastor explained the way of salvation to the man the same evening. 'I went from that church "a new creature".' But this man also expressed his view that, humanly speaking, 'if there had not been an appeal that night, I would probably have gone home and that would have been the end of it.' That was over forty-two years ago. The man is the Rev. Arthur Thompson, a leader of London Baptists (General Superintendent of the Metropolitan Area).

The Rev. Gavin Reid put it like this. The opportunity for people to respond to the preaching of the gospel by coming out to the front allows people 'to do what they *want* to do, not to make them do what they don't want to do'. It is true that such an opportunity has been abused by ministers who wanted to appear 'successful' by the number of people who openly respond. But what a pity if we throw out the baby with the bath water. There is a valid time and place for giving men, women, boys and girls an opportunity to respond to what they have heard. I believe the time for such is at the close of an evangelistic sermon and that the place for it is right in the church.

I have come across a good number of people who have admitted to realising over the years that they are no doubt Christians but remained largely in hiding. Their own growth, not to mention assurance, might have been greatly helped and encouraged had there been an opportunity to respond openly at a definite time and place. One needs to be committed and know for oneself that one is committed. When we respond before a gathering of people, we help prove to ourselves whether or not we are in earnest about confessing Christ and following Him.

· People will *want* to respond in some way if they believe what they have heard. I don't think that Simon Peter was prepared for the response he was going to get when he preached his sermon on the day of Pentecost. But the impact of his message was most profound on the hearts of his hearers. For they were cut to the heart and cried out to Peter, 'What shall we do?' (Acts 2: 37). Peter told them to repent and then be baptised – a public pledge. Then we are told that Peter had more to say to his listeners. '*With many other words* did he testify and exhort, saying, Save yourselves from this untoward generation' (Acts 2: 40). As Dr O. S. Hawkins has pointed out, if that was not the equivalent of calling men and women forward, what was it? The phrase 'save yourselves' is a forgotten phrase among Peter's words that day. It is a phrase that might embarrass some. But there is no doubt in my mind that Peter was doing the very same thing as this book is calling for.

If we ministers today would not be afraid to say to people, 'Save yourselves', we too might have a greater response to our preaching. Moreover, when we say to men, 'Save yourselves', they are going to want assurance that they are saving themselves. Allowing people to make a public pledge by walking forward provides this assurance. On the day of Pentecost they wasted no time. 'Those who accepted his message were baptised, and about 3,000 were added to their number *that day*' (Acts 2: 41, NIV). How much these 3,000 grasped is not known. Whether all were truly regenerated is not known. But those who gladly received Peter's word were *baptised* – right on the spot (or somewhere not too far away). There was no testing period, no trial period, no period of probation, no waiting to see whether they were 'genuine'. That kind of fear did not enter the disciples' minds. They just baptised all that accepted the message. What a day it was!

And what a day it is when one witnesses the same thing, even if in smaller numbers. Just to see a person walk forward is a thrilling sight! Let the cynics scoff, let them say, 'It won't last'. Arthur Thompson said to me of the night he responded, 'Friends said that it would wear off, but forty-two years later I can gladly say that He who delivered me in 1942 is still delivering me in 1984.' And what if it *did* 'wear off'? Was the pastor who invited people to make a public response in the wrong? No. It was the Pharisees who were annoyed that people were shouting 'Hosanna!' to Jesus on Palm Sunday. They were particularly irritated that children got in on this praise. But Jesus said, 'Have you never read, "From the lips of children and infants you have ordained praise"?' (Matt. 21:16, NIV). It can further be pointed out that these same people apparently deserted Jesus by Good Friday. But Jesus not only affirmed their Palm Sunday response to Him but said, 'I tell you that, if these should hold their peace, the stones would immediately cry out' (Luke 19:40). Jesus even endorsed their emotional response. Indeed, I do not believe that God is offended over a person walking forward in response to the message, even though he has not truly been converted. A young preacher said to Mr Spurgeon, 'But what if we convert one of the non-elect?' Spurgeon replied, patting the man on the shoulder, 'God will forgive you for that.'

The presentation of the gospel now called Evangelism Explosion includes a call for an immediate response if the listener claims that what he has heard makes sense to him. This is part of its genius. One evening I watched Dr D. James Kennedy present the gospel to an architect who had a home on the coast in Fort Lauderdale. This dignified, aristocratic-looking gentleman was at first upset because we even knocked on the door of his home. That didn't bother Dr Kennedy. During the thirty-minute presentation of the gospel I watched that man sink deeper and deeper into his plush couch. When Dr Kennedy finished, he said to the man, 'Does this make sense to you?' 'Yes, it does,' replied this man. Dr Kennedy then proceeded to show this man that this 'eternal life' is a 'gift' and that a 'gift must be received'. Thus Dr Kennedy asked, 'Do you want to receive this gift?' The man did. A year later I asked Dr Kennedy about that man. 'Oh, didn't I tell you about him? He's now a *trainer* in the Evangelism Explosion programme.' Not all who respond immediately turn out so well. But in one sense that does not matter. The call for an immediate response is biblical and glorifying to God.

This book, therefore, should have relevance both for the minister and the layman. As a layman you should never hesitate to invite a man to receive Christ right on the spot if you have witnessed to him. You may be surprised how much he *wants* to do something as soon as he has heard the good news. Furthermore, by inviting him to pray to receive Christ then and there – even if he doesn't – presses home to him that this is what he should do! The call for a response accentuates the importance of a man being converted – changed. Not a few of those Arthur Blessitt has led to Jesus Christ have heard the gospel only briefly. I sometimes wonder if more people will be in heaven who were won to the Lord by Arthur Blessitt on a one-to-one basis than by any other man in the history of the Christian Church. I learned a few days ago of a young lady who wandered on to Sunset Strip in Hollywood, having run away from home. She ran into Arthur who gave her the gospel and led her to Christ. Arthur never saw her again. He received a letter from her, however, years later – from behind the Iron Curtain. The young lady was now a missionary. 'I've been trying to find your address for years,' she said.

Anybody can lead a soul to Jesus Christ. What is often underestimated is the need for a person to respond to the gospel *at once*. It is the minister's high privilege to provide an opportunity to do this before he finishes his sermon. The call for people of all ages to pledge themselves publicly to Jesus allows them to do what they want to do. They deserve an opportunity to respond. They should not be turned away by our letting them go back into the cold, dark world where nobody else will ever be likely to confront them with the claims of Jesus Christ. Moreover, should a person have responded publicly to the gospel and it turned out to be the last time he heard the gospel, what consolation it is for the friends and loved ones to know of this response. After all, the alternative to believing the gospel is to remain in a state of condemnation. 'Whoever believes in him is not condemned, but whoever does not believe stands condemned already' (John 3:18, NIV). What one does in response to the gospel changes one's eternal destiny; calling for a person to respond *now* is but the reasonable thing to do in the light of eternity.

I should like to think that this very book could be the means of leading a person to Jesus Christ. Admittedly this is not primarily addressed to the non-Christian. But a reader may look through these pages who knows in his heart that he is not really born again. I would hate to think that a book like this would not be adequate to lead a person to a saving knowledge of Christ. I should hope that the clarity of the gospel will be obvious and that the urgency to confess Christ as Lord and Saviour will impel *you* to make your calling and election sure. Confessing Jesus Christ openly is what *ratifies* a person's interest in Jesus Christ. To ratify means *to give validity to*. It is like the signature at the bottom of a letter. Thus a person may believe in his heart without confessing to what he believes. This is why Paul said, 'For it is with your heart that you believe and are justified, and it is with your mouth that you *confess and are saved*' (Romans 10:10, NIV).

No, coming out to the front of the church is not the only way of coming out of hiding. You can confess Christ and ratify the promise of your own salvation by telling one other person. It does not matter who you tell – your wife, husband, parent, sister, son or daughter, friend, neighbour, or stranger! Tell it to one other person. On the other hand, the more you confess to the better. Doing it before a rather large gathering takes more courage but it could mean a greater victory for you – not to mention what it does for all who look on. But do not think that coming forward as I recommend is the only way you confess Jesus Christ openly.

But perhaps we are getting ahead of the story. Are you saved? Do you know for certain that if you were to die one hour from now you would go to heaven? One of the reasons that the Bible was written was that you may 'know that you have eternal life' (1 John 5:13, NIV). Do you know this? Moreover, suppose you were to stand before God and He were to ask you, 'Why should I let you into my heaven?' what would you say? If you have never thought about a question like this, why not lay this book aside for a moment and write on a slip of paper what your answer to this last question is – then come back to the book, continue reading and compare your answer with what I submit below.

Perhaps you would like to know what many others have said in answer to that question. 'I have tried to live a good life.' 'I believe in the Ten Commandments.' 'I try to keep the Golden Rule.' 'I have never hurt anybody.' 'I walked forward at a Billy Graham crusade.' 'I was baptised.' 'I joined the Church.' 'I was brought up in a Christian home.' 'I'm as good as the next person.' 'I believe in God.' 'I like going to church.' 'Please God, let me in.' 'I love you.' 'I've tried to be a good husband/wife/parent.' 'I knelt at an altar.'

Nearly all of the above answers begin with 'I' and stress what the person has done to *earn* his way into heaven. If your own answer is similar to one of those above, you are like most people in thinking that we get to heaven by our good works. But now for the good news. That is what the word 'gospel' means – good news! Heaven is a *free gift*. It is not earned or merited by anything we have done. 'For it is by grace you have been saved, through faith – and this not from yourselves, it is the *gift* of God – not by works, so that no one can boast' (Eph. 2:8–9, NIV). 'For the wages of sin is death, but the *gift* of God is eternal life in Christ Jesus our Lord' (Rom. 6:23, NIV).

It may surprise you that heaven is given to you absolutely freely, but that is the only way it could be. For the standard of entrance into heaven is so high that none of us can attain to it. The Bible even says that if we keep the whole law and yet stumble at one point, we are guilty of breaking all of it (Jas. 2:10). We see this more clearly when we realise what the Bible says about man – us. We are sinners. 'All have sinned and fall short of the glory of God' (Rom. 3:23, NIV). You are a sinner. I am a sinner. We do not have to rob a bank, murder a person or commit adultery in order to sin. Jesus said that to be angry with another is murder and that 'anyone who looks at a woman lustfully has already committed adultery with her in his heart' (Matt. 5:22,27, NIV). It is actually possible to sin by doing nothing! I can prove it. Jesus said that the greatest commandment is to 'Love the Lord your God with all your heart and with all your soul and with all your mind' (Matt. 22:37, NIV). Not to do that is not only to sin but to sin against the greatest commandment. We are all sinners. If we go to heaven, it will be because God simply *gives* it to us. We could never earn it. But the problem becomes even more acute when we realise what the Bible says about God. The Bible basically says two things about God – that He is merciful and that He is just. By merciful it means that God does not want to punish us. He does not want anyone to perish (2 Pet. 3:9). 'The Lord is compassionate and gracious, slow to anger, abounding in love' (Ps. 103: 8, NIV). But God is also just. This means that He must punish sin. 'He does not leave the guilty unpunished' (Exod. 34: 7, NIV). His eyes are 'too pure to look on evil' or to 'tolerate wrong' (Hab. 1: 13, NIV). 'The wrath of God is being revealed from heaven against all the godlessness and wickedness of men' (Rom. 1: 18, NIV).

In other words, the Bible says that God is *both* merciful and just. Have you any idea how God can be just and merciful at the same time? The answer is: His mercy and justice came together in the person of Jesus Christ. God sent His Son Jesus Christ – God in the flesh. 'In the beginning was the Word, and the Word was with God, and the Word was God' (John 1:1). For in Christ all the fulness of the Godhead lives 'in bodily form' (Col. 2: 9, NIV). On

Good Friday Jesus was crucified. While Jesus was hanging on the cross, all of the sins of the world were transferred to Him – as though He Himself was guilty. 'The Lord has laid on him the iniquity of us all' (Isa. 53: 6, NIV). What that means is this. God punished Jesus for *our* sins. God's justice was thus satisfied when Jesus died for our sins. A verse I quoted above says that the 'wages of sin is death' (Rom. 6: 23). Jesus never sinned, so He ought not to have died. Why *did* He die? He was smitten by God. 'He was pierced for our transgressions, he was crushed for our iniquities' (Isa. 53: 4-5, NIV). 'God made him who had no sin to be sin for us' (2 Cor. 5: 21, NIV).

In a word: God punished Jesus for our sins that He might be merciful to us. That is how He could be just and merciful at the same time. Just before Jesus died, He uttered the words, 'It is finished' (John 19: 30). In the original Greek it is the word *tetelestai* – an ancient expression in the market place for 'paid in full'. When Jesus died on the cross, He paid our debt – in full. He bought us a place in heaven by His death on the cross. It is therefore through His death that eternal life is offered freely to us.

We receive this gift by faith. By faith I mean *saving* faith. I put it like that for this reason. There is a faith that is not necessarily saving faith. 'You believe that there is one God. Good! Even the demons believe that – and shudder' (James 2:19, NIV). There is a faith that one might call crisis faith. Many cry out to God when they are in trouble. General Douglas McArthur used to say that there are no atheists in foxholes. But that is not saving faith. There is also intellectual faith – assent to certain doctrines of the Church about God and Christ. But belief in these doctrines will not save you.

Saving faith is when you *transfer* all the trust you have in yourself – your good works, etc. – to Jesus Christ alone. Saving faith is *trusting Jesus Christ alone*. Therefore if God were to ask me, 'Why should I let you into my heaven?' I would reply, 'Because Jesus died on the cross for my sins. That is my only hope.'

You may receive this gift by faith – right where you are. You do not need to wait until Sunday. You may call on God this very moment. In your heart I would urge you now to pray this prayer: 'Dear God, I know I am a sinner. I am sorry for my sins. I repent of my sins. I believe that Jesus is the Son of God and that He died on the cross for my sins. Wash away my sins by His precious blood. I now welcome your Holy Spirit into my heart. As best as I know how, I give you my life. Amen.'

What remains for you to do is to come out of hiding. You must confess that you have trusted Jesus Christ. 'Whoever acknowledges me before men, I will also acknowledge him before my Father in heaven' (Matt. 10:32, NIV). 'If anyone is ashamed of me and my words in this adulterous and sinful generation, the Son of Man will be ashamed of him when he comes in his Father's glory with the holy angels' (Mark 8:38, NIV). 'It is with your mouth that you confess and are saved' (Rom. 10:10, NIV).

Coming out of hiding is only the beginning. The Bible says, 'Be filled with the Spirit' (Eph. 5:18). You must pray daily. Read the Bible daily. Witness for Christ daily. Attend a church where the Bible is preached and Christ is honoured. Keep Christ's commandments. The reason for this is that you should 'grow in the grace and knowledge of our Lord and Saviour Jesus Christ' (2 Pet. 3:18, NIV).

Perhaps you have heard (and believed) that religion is a very personal matter – that you should keep it to yourself. That may be true with religion. But not salvation. God calls men to confess His Son before everybody. If salvation by Jesus Christ were merely a 'personal matter', Christianity would have died in the first generation. But Paul could say to the people that were saved in Thessalonica, 'The Lord's message rang out from you not only in Macedonia and Achaia – your faith in God has become known everywhere' (I Thess. 1:8, NIV). Paul could say to Christians in Rome – right under the shadow of the Caesar, 'I thank my God through Jesus Christ for all of you, because your faith is being reported all over the world' (Rom. 1:8, NIV). 'Everyone has heard about your obedience, so I am full of joy over you' (Rom. 16:19, NIV).

If you really believe in your heart that Jesus Christ is the Son of God, how can you keep quiet about it? You cannot. This is why confession ratifies what is in the heart – thus proving that it *is* in the heart indeed. You sign your name to a letter because you are not ashamed of what you have written. You confess Jesus Christ with your mouth because you are not ashamed of what you have believed. Confession without the belief in the heart will not save, however. This is why coming forward does not save anybody. Something must happen in the heart. But if it does happen in the heart, you are required to prove that by your confession. Your refusal to confess Christ openly casts serious doubt on whether you really believe in the Lord Jesus Christ in your heart.

I therefore do not call on anyone to do what he does not want to do. The call to stand up and be counted is to enable people to do what they want to do, not make them do what they don't want to do.

The call to stand up and be counted is God's pledge to you that 'Everyone who trusts in (Jesus) will never be put to shame' (Rom. 10: 11, NIV). That is God's promise to all of us. The very call, then, to stand up and be counted is *God's* pledge that He will not disown you if you demonstrate that you are not ashamed of Him. Your confession before men is your pledge to God and man that you are unashamed of Jesus Christ and that you believe He died on the cross for your sins and rose from the dead. By 'going public' with this pledge, you send a signal to the world that you belong to God. But you also allow them the privilege of watching you from now on as well. You cannot confess the Lord with your mouth without suggesting to others that they watch your life.

Are you ready to stand up and be counted? If you have not done it, do it now. It is your privilege.

2

THE PUBLIC PLEDGE:
ITS ROOTS, SHOOTS AND FRUITS

> 'But Abram said to the king of Sodom, "I have raised
> my hand to the Lord, God Most High, Creator of
> heaven and earth, and have taken an oath that I will
> accept nothing belonging to you, not even a thread or
> the thong of a sandal, so that you will never be able to
> say, 'I made Abram rich'."' (Gen. 14:22–3, NIV)

All of us feel more comfortable with any practice which
has its roots in undoubted antiquity. This is especially
true in Britain where tradition plays an important part in
one's thinking. I suspect that in America there is a greater
receptivity to what is novel or innovative, but it is not like
that in Britain. Tradition over here is very important, and
the older the tradition, the weightier the idea or practice
involved.

One of the biggest obstacles I have faced on the subject
of tithing is precisely this. The preaching of tithing,
speaking generally, is not common in Britain. This is why
I felt a book on the subject was timely. As for tradition,
then, it was not decidedly on my side when I broached the
subject of tithing. I built my case on the Bible.

So with the subject at hand. Tradition is not on our side.
If I could show that the practice of calling people to the
front before the final benediction of the service was carried
out by Archbishop Thomas Cranmer or Bishop Hugh
Latimer, by George Whitefield or John Wesley – or even

C. H. Spurgeon, my task would be easy (and this book possibly would not have been conceived). The difficulty is that it is chiefly regarded as an American import. But the same thing has been said with regard to the emphasis on tithing.

And yet my present task is somewhat more difficult than making the case for tithing. With tithing one has the biblical *word* to start with and its origin in the meeting between Abraham and Melchizedek. But with the subject of this book I have had to coin a phrase that has no exact biblical text.

Having no scriptural verse that explicitly refers to public pledge, our task is to look for the biblical equivalent. I was to discover, as I began this book, that the public pledge also had some roots in the meeting between Abraham and Melchizedek.

God first began calling people out of hiding in the garden of Eden. Immediately after Adam and Eve ate the forbidden fruit, 'the eyes of them both were opened, and they knew that they were naked'. They thus sewed fig leaves together and made coverings for themselves. Then they heard the voice of the Lord God in the cool of the day, 'and Adam and his wife hid themselves from the presence of the Lord God amongst the trees of the garden' (Gen. 3:7–8). Sin always leads one to retreat into hiding. 'And this is the condemnation, that light is come into the world, and men loved darkness rather than light, because their deeds were evil' (John 3:19). The task of every minister is to address men and women in this wilful darkness and hiding. That is what God did in Eden. 'And the Lord God called unto Adam, and said unto him, Where art thou?' (Gen. 3:9).

No public pledge followed on Adam's part. Only self-justification. 'The woman whom thou gavest to be with me, she gave me of the tree, and I did eat' (Gen. 3:12). Adam blamed Eve and Eve blamed the serpent. 'The serpent beguiled me, and I did eat' (Gen. 3:13). But Adam and Eve, though called out of hiding and provided with garments of skin by God Himself (Gen. 3:21), were given no opportunity that we know of to make any kind of pledge to God.

I will not elaborate on the possibility that Abel's offering was some sort of pledge to God (Gen. 4:4) or what may be implied by the reference to the time men began 'to call upon the name of the Lord' (Gen. 4:26). It could have been a public demonstration. But we may be sure that Noah's obedience was open and obvious before everybody. God told him to make an ark with definite specifications that must have made him feel like an utter fool before his generation. But what we know is that whatever God required, 'Thus did Noah: according to all that God commanded him, so did he' (Gen. 6:22). That was certainly public.

When God said to Abram, 'Get thee out of thy country, and from thy kindred' (Gen. 12:1), this was a call to come out of hiding. Abraham had been a sun worshipper. He was called out of darkness into light. This moreover required a public commitment in that this obedience was not done in a corner. 'So Abram departed, as the Lord had spoken unto him; and Lot went with him' (Gen. 12:4). Abraham 'went out, not knowing whither he went' (Heb. 11:8). This was public. But there is no indication of a pledge on Abraham's part.

The first account in the Old Testament that has the ingredients of what we are calling public pledge took place immediately following Abraham's meeting with Melchizedek. The story is this. Abraham's nephew Lot, who foolishly had pitched his tent towards Sodom (Gen. 13:12), got caught in the cross-fire of a war between the king of Sodom and other kings. Lot ended up losing both his possessions and his freedom. Word of this got back to Abraham, who at once proceeded to rescue his nephew. The success of Abraham (with 318 of his trained men) in defeating all the kings was phenomenal. Not only did Abraham subdue the kings and plunder them but also rescued Lot in the meantime, recovering all his goods together with the women and the other people. At this point there emerges one of the more mysterious and

sublime events in all Holy Writ. Out of the blue one called
Melchizedek, 'king of Salem and priest of the Most High
God', brought out bread and wine and blessed Abraham,
saying 'Blessed be Abram by God Most High, Creator of
heaven and earth. And blessed be God Most High, who
delivered your enemies into your hand' (Gen. 14:19–20,
NIV). It is at this point that tithing comes into the picture.
Abraham gave Melchizedek 'tithes of all' (Gen. 14:20).

Furthermore the king of Sodom, no doubt grateful to
Abraham, said to him, 'Give me the people and keep the
goods for yourself' (Gen. 14:21, NIV). This is when
Abraham responded with the words quoted above at the
beginning of this chapter. I find it fascinating that this
comment should appear not only in the life of Abraham
but at this particular juncture. I admit that there is a
danger of pressing this too far, but there are no fewer than
ten ingredients of our public pledge that are found in
Abraham's statement that will bear our looking into.

1. What Abraham said to the king of Sodom was a *pledge*.
'I have raised my hand to the Lord . . . and have taken an
oath.' A pledge is the earnest token of one's sincerity or
truthfulness. That is precisely the point Abraham wanted
to make in this meeting with the king of Sodom. Abraham
says that he has taken an 'oath'.

2. It was *public*. Who besides the king of Sodom was
present is not known. But there can be little doubt that this
was an astonishing testimony before a king of a godless
country that Abram would speak as he did. What is
absolutely certain is that there was nothing secret about
Abraham's commitment.

3. It was Abraham's *personal decision*. He gave no hint
that this was anything but his own voluntary choice. 'I
have raised my hand.' He did what he did because it was
what he wanted to do.

4. The pledge was not only before the world but *before*

God. 'I have raised my hand to the Lord, God Most High.'
Abraham knew that what he was doing was glorifying to
God. He knew that God was looking on. It was not only a
testimony before a godless king but it was a conscious,
deliberate act before God.

5. The pledge shows that Abraham was not only
unashamed of his testimony but that he wanted to be
identified with the true God. 'I have raised my hand to the
Lord, God Most High, Creator of heaven and earth.' A
public pledge is necessarily an identification with the true
God and all that He claims for Himself.

6. Abraham obviously believed all that he affirmed in his
heart. Any confession must be rooted in the heart. 'If you
confess with your mouth, "Jesus is Lord", and believe in
your heart that God raised him from the dead, you will be
saved' (Rom. 10:9, NIV). What Abraham did before God
and the king of Sodom sprang from his heart.

7. There is no hint that Abraham thought he was
righteous because he made this confession. He was not
trying to earn anything by this. He was not trying to 'score
points' with God. This line of thinking did not apparently
enter his mind.

8. This pledge was made *immediately following* his
encounter with Melchizedek – a 'type' of Christ. Who
Melchizedek really was in a sense does not matter, but the
writer of the Epistle to the Hebrews says that he was 'like'
the Son of God (Heb. 7:3). Melchizedek was like Jesus in
no fewer than three ways: (1) In his three-fold office:
prophet, priest, king. He thus anticipated all that Jesus
was. (2) Melchizedek bringing out bread and wine to
Abraham points to the death of Jesus on the cross in much
the same way as did the institution of the Lord's Supper.
(3) The reference to Melchizedek in Psalm 110:4, according
to Hebrews 5:5-10, points to the resurrection, ascension
and continuous intercession of Christ at God's right hand.

9. As a pledge equally points to a commitment that goes beyond the present moment, Abraham vowed to the king of Sodom, 'I will not take from a thread even to a shoelatchet, and that I will not take any thing that is thine, lest thou shouldest say, I have made Abram rich' (Gen. 14:23). Abraham's pledge works good for the future as well as the present.

10. Abraham's public pledge implies a separation from the world. Abraham clearly wanted to be distinguished from the king of Sodom. 'Lest thou shouldest say, I have made Abram rich.' Abraham clearly wanted it to go on record that his debt was to God alone and that he did not want to give the king of Sodom any hope that the blessing, or success, was to be attributed in some way to the world.

What is meant in this book by public pledge is set forth almost more clearly in these ten observations than anything else that could be said. If it is countered that Abraham was not specifically invited by anybody to come forward with this public pledge but that it was wholly spontaneous, I answer: so was his decision to tithe. As tithing is giving people the privilege of doing what they want to do – the Lord loves a cheerful giver – so also the public pledge gives them the privilege of doing what they want to do. But it does not follow that we should leave all righteous obedience to 'spontaneous combustion'. What often begins spontaneously must be continued diligently. Some of us want to opt out of obedience because it is not spontaneous. But this is wrong. It is irresponsible. This is also why tithing must be preached. It would be an irresponsible minister who urged people to do what is right only when they 'feel' like it.

Many years ago I felt somewhat prompted to arise at a certain hour to pray. I said, 'Lord, if you really want me to get up at this hour, you wake me up. That way I will know you really want me to do it.' I can tell you that the very next morning I found myself wide awake. My first reaction was to try to go back to sleep. I looked at my watch. It was dead on the exact hour I had asked to be awakened. As a matter of fact it was the time that made me remember that I had asked the Lord to wake me up at that hour! I was actually surprised. So I got up and spent the time in prayer. On the same evening as I was getting ready to go to bed I prayed, 'Lord, do it again. Wake me up at the same hour.' I can tell you, I slept past that hour by two hours! I tried for several successive nights to get the Lord (rather than the alarm clock) to wake me up, but it never happened again. I now use a good alarm clock. Always.

Spontaneity is often the way God begins something which He wants to continue. But if it is right, then it is worth doing regularly and with effort. As I have said elsewhere, if I waited until I felt 'led' to pray, I doubt I'd pray very much. 'Every time I feel the Spirit moving in my heart I'll pray,' says the old spiritual. But it isn't spiritual people who adopt that line of thinking. We should do something because it has a valid biblical precedent not because we are given the 'luxury' of spontaneity to do the same thing. If it is right to do when there is 'much' (power, spontaneity and effortlessness), it is right to do when there is 'least' (struggle, effort and self-control).

The essential elements of the public pledge can be seen to run right through the Bible. God always wants His people to demonstrate that they are not ashamed of Him. Those God has used most and with whom He has been most familiar have been those that openly demonstrate their love to God. This is why the public pledge is honouring to God and it is why He has blessed its use when it is not abused. Jacob demonstrated how grateful he was for God's presence by changing the name of a city! After the vision of the ladder with angels ascending and descending it Jacob said, 'The Lord is in this place; and I knew it not.' He got up the next morning, took the stone he had placed under his head and set it up as a pillar and poured oil on top of it. 'And he called the name of that place Bethel: but the name of that city was called Luz at the first' (Gen. 28:19).

The public pledge was even demonstrated by King

Pharaoh. After Joseph interpreted Pharaoh's dream – which nobody else could interpret – and then gave some application as to what the king ought to do in the light of the interpretation, Pharaoh agreed. He not only agreed but he affirmed Joseph right on the spot! Pharaoh took off his ring and put it on Joseph's finger, then put a gold chain around his neck and let him ride in a chariot as Pharaoh's second-in-command. All this because he *believed Joseph's word!* Joseph had forecast seven years of plenty to be followed by seven years of leanness – the interpretation of the king's dream. He then recommended to the king that the first seven years be spent in storing up for the seven bad years to come.

Pharaoh might easily have said to Joseph, 'Thank you very much. You have given me an interesting interpretation of my dream and you have given some sensible advice. But I cannot be sure that you are right or that all this is really going to happen. We will wait and see.' But no. Pharaoh believed Joseph's words on the spot and put his own honour and credibility on the line by publicly accepting the word of a Hebrew prisoner. *Everybody* knew what Pharaoh had done – without waiting to see how things would turn out. It could not have been more public: to the new prime minister they cried, 'Bow the knee' (Gen. 41:43).

I was preaching from this very text on a Sunday evening in November 1982. I came to the point in the sermon, perhaps half-way through, and simply made the application that those who become Christians must put themselves on the line just as Pharaoh had done. I stressed that we must not wait until we see how things work out; we must confess the Lord *now* and show *now* that we are unashamed and that we really do believe His *word.* I then said in my sermon, 'Are you ashamed of Jesus Christ?' All of a sudden a six-foot-six-inch young man, about twelve rows back, stood up and shouted, 'No!' I looked at him and noticed an earnest and determined countenance. I could see he was not a heckler. I turned to him and said, 'You're confessing Christ right now, aren't you?' He nodded

affirmatively. I said, 'Very well. You may now sit down.'
At the close of the service he was the first to go out to the
front of the church. I have since baptised this man and
have got to know him. He is by temperament a very shy
fellow. But he said to me, 'Had I not stood up at that
moment, I do believe I would have burst.' I must add that
we did not have this kind of liberty and power in the
services at Westminster before I began calling people to
the front.

The most painful decision that a man ever made was
when Moses, aged forty, 'refused to be called the son of
Pharaoh's daughter' but chose instead to suffer affliction
with the people of God. He actually esteemed the
'reproach of Christ' as having greater value than the
treasures of Egypt (Heb. 11:24–6). That is the way this man
declared himself. There was nothing secret about it. Forty
years later he instructed the children of Israel to sprinkle
blood over and on the sides of the doors of their homes.
The night of the Passover was a visible demonstration of
their obedience – it was a public pledge. It was their pledge
to God and God's pledge to them and it was their witness
before the world. And God said, 'When I see the blood, I
will pass over you' (Exod. 12:13). The One in whom this
Passover ordinance would be fulfilled was later to say,
'Whosoever therefore shall confess me before men, him
will I confess also before my Father which is in heaven'
(Matt. 10:32).

After the children of Israel crossed the Red Sea and were
wandering in the wilderness, there was a fresh need for
commitment. One might regard this incident as a
justification for *recommitment* – publicly. I tend not to
push this too hard in Westminster or the most sensitive
souls will come to the front every week. But there was a
time when Moses addressed the children of Israel with
these words, 'Who is on the Lord's side? let him come unto
me. And all the sons of Levi gathered themselves together
unto him' (Exod. 32:26).

After Moses died, his successor Joshua addressed the
children of Israel in yet another time of spiritual crisis.

'Choose you this day whom ye will serve.' The people responded, 'We will serve the Lord.' Joshua then asked for a public demonstration of their commitment (Josh. 24:15-27). An open demonstration of one's heart – a public pledge – is a consistent strain in the Bible.

John the Baptist came preaching in the wilderness of Judaea. Those receiving John's message confessed their sins and made this repentance public by being baptised. But John was not prepared for one person who asked to be baptised, Jesus, who had come all the way from Galilee. John tried to deter him. 'I need to be baptised by you, and do you come to me?' Jesus insisted that John baptise Him – 'to fulfil all righteousness'. Then John consented (Matt. 3:6,13-15).

A lot more is contained in those words 'fulfil all righteousness' than can be explored here. But truly, if we are to follow in the steps of our Lord who 'knew no sin' (2 Cor. 5:21), how much more should we do what He did?

Baptism was the public pledge of John's day and has always been the manner in which a person confesses Jesus Christ. But without wishing to open up the whole subject of baptism, I would have thought that the main point is: one must respond publicly to the preached word. John baptised at Aenon near Salim because there was plenty of water (John 3:23), but when there is not plenty of water, there should none the less be an opportunity for people to respond to what they hear. This is why I have said that the public pledge *temporarily* takes the place of baptism.

One reason why the same people who come forward ought also to be baptised, apart from the fact that walking to the front is obviously not baptism, is because they can plan ahead for their baptism and can invite their friends to witness it. This way it becomes a planned testimony to conversion whereas walking to the front will probably have been spontaneous. At Westminster Chapel the baptistry, built by G. Campbell Morgan a long time ago, is not conveniently located nor is it easy to fill with water. We therefore have baptismal services several times a year as needed – not every week. But it does not mean that one cannot openly confess Christ at the Chapel every week.

In the second quarter of the eighteenth century a phenomenon now called the Great Awakening emerged on both sides of the Atlantic. It was by no means the first extraordinary work of God in church history since the days of the earliest disciples. God was doing mighty things with the church fathers (e.g. Chrysostom, Athanasius, Augustine), not to mention God's Holy Spirit at work in the Great Reformation (e.g. Luther, the English re-formers, Calvin). But the way in which God chose to work in the eighteenth century was in many ways un-precedented (as far as I am able to discover). The preaching of the gospel literally struck men to the ground with such conviction that some were unconscious for a while, and others not so struck down were left in a terrible agony with regard to the state of their souls. In some cases those not struck down were terrified at the thought that there might not be any hope for them. The result was a general seeking after God and a most intense concern for assurance of salvation. The chief preachers during those days were John Wesley and George Whitefield in England and Jonathan Edwards in America.

But there were other preachers in America that are not as well known. Many people have heard of Dartmouth College and many Baptists will know the name Isaac Backus, who was a Baptist historian and champion of religious liberty. Less known is Eleazar Wheelock. Wheelock was a Congregational minister who became the founder and first president of Dartmouth. He was a chief instrument also in the conversion of Isaac Backus in 1741. But even less known is the fact that Eleazar Wheelock, as best as I am able to pinpoint, is the first person in modern times to call people to the front of the church in order to seek the Lord.

The year was 1741, when by all accounts the Great Awakening was at flood tide. The Spirit of God was at work powerfully in New England, especially in Connecti-cut. In Enfield Jonathan Edwards preached his famous sermon 'Sinners in the hands of an angry God'. But not far away – in Lebanon, Connecticut – Eleazar Wheelock was preaching. An eyewitness gave this report:

> As he was delivering his discourse very pleasantly and moderately, the depth and strength of feeling increased, till some began to cry out both above and below, in awful distress and anguish of soul, upon which he raised his voice, that he might be heard above their outcries; but the distress and outcry spreading and increasing, his voice was at length so drowned that he could not be heard. Wherefore, not being able to finish his sermon, with great apparent serenity and calmness of soul, he called to the distressed, and desired them to gather themselves together in the body of the seats below. This he did, that he might the more conveniently converse with them, counsel, direct, exhort them, etc. But he ought not to have done it . . . He should have sent his hearers home, to engage in solitary, serious thought, in reading.

What is of particular interest is that the one describing this scene was not too happy with Wheelock's desire to call the distressed to 'the body of the seats below'. For this eyewitness offered his own opinion that Wheelock 'ought not to have done it'. This suggests that (1) the practice was probably not widely accepted in 1741, (2) the eyewitness was fearful that Wheelock might bring these distressed persons to premature profession or assurance, and (3) that the Holy Spirit alone should lead a person to assurance without the counsel or guidance of a human instrument.

But what interests me also is this: the modern practice of calling people to the front (or whatever 'the body of the seats below' means) was apparently born in authentic revival. An unusual work of the Spirit of God was going on in New England in 1741. The description above of Wheelock's preaching sounds very like eyewitness reports of Jonathan Edwards's aforementioned sermon. There is no report (that I know of) that Edwards did what Wheelock did, but what is well known is that Edwards had to pause in his sermon because of the audible groans of his congregation and pointedly asked them to try to restrain themselves so that he could finish. In a word: the same power of the Spirit was present in Wheelock's service as was present in that of Jonathan Edwards. It was undoubtedly exactly the same intensity of conviction on the audience. But in Wheelock's case he did what might well have been – although it is not proven – unprecedented.

This to me is weighty. The very practice of the minister calling people to the front – by whatever name – was born in true revival. It was not born in a time of dryness. It was not born at a time when people were trying to manipulate people. The practice started in undoubted revival. What do you do with anxious souls? Do you pray with them, or follow the opinion of the above eyewitness – and leave them alone?

This leads me to another thing that interests me about this 1741 account. I am impressed with a man who had the pastoral sensitivity to call people forward in order to help them. Wheelock was not thinking of how many people he could have at the front. I seriously doubt that this thought entered his mind. It seems to me that there was nothing in his mind but the care of souls. What is more impressive is that the account was drawn up by a rather unsympathetic witness. A sympathetic witness might have been tempted to embellish the story. What is obvious is that Wheelock could see these people were in trouble. Knowing the theology and climate of the day, we can safely assume that these people were afraid they were among the reprobate – the non-elect, who were predestined to damnation. Issac Backus records in his diary that he himself was afraid that he was among the damned who could never experience conversion. This man Wheelock had a pastoral heart. That is why he called men to the front. To encourage them.

The modern practice of calling people forward began in real revival. You could say that it had a spontaneous beginning.

I have talked with some experts on the period in question who have said they would not be surprised if the 'mourner's bench' or 'anxious seat' was used on either side of the Atlantic during the eighteenth century. But I cannot prove this. Nor can they. A pastor-scholar by the name of Edward Norris Kirk, pastor of the Mount Vernon Church in Boston (1868–74) and who lectured at Andover Newton in the 1860s took it for granted that the anxious seat was common in Wesley's day. He refers to a line of Charles Wesley, 'Oh that blessed anxious seat', in one of his lectures. But he does not give his source. I have not found the origin. As Charles Wesley wrote 6,000 hymns, it would be like looking for a needle in a haystack. It is also possible that Wesley meant something other than what Kirk was implying, even if he did say it. Perhaps a reader can provide the source and shed some light on this.

But the literature that is available which describes what was going on at the turn of the century (1799–1800) gives the impression that the call for people to seek the Lord by stepping out to the front (to kneel or sit) was not regarded as unusual. It seems to have been going on before.

I come now to the Cane Ridge revival. It took place on the banks of the Red River in Logan County, Kentucky, a few miles north of the Tennessee border. The year was 1800. A 'camp meeting' was in progress. (It would seem that the camp meeting phenomenon actually began in 1799 on the banks of the Red River. People came in covered waggons for miles to meet for worship and Christian fellowship.) It is estimated that at one point at least 20,000 people were present. An eyewitness (writing in 1802) said that some had come 200 miles and that at least 140 waggons came loaded with people. This witness also wrote:

> People began to fall down... This was a new thing among Presbyterians: it excited universal astonishment, and created a curiosity which could not be restrained when people fell during the most solemn parts of divine service... at Cane Ridge they met on Friday and

continued till Wednesday evening, night and day
without intermission, either in the public or private
exercises of devotion; and with such earnestness that
heavy showers were not sufficient to disperse them . . . so
many Deists constrained to call on the formerly despised
name of Jesus . . . [at one point] not less than 1,000
persons fell prostrate to the ground, among whom were
many infidels . . . persons falling down [were] carried
out of the crowd, by those next to them, and taken to
some convenient place, where prayer is made for them.

Those who fell down are said to have become 'totally
powerless' just immediately before they fell. Others not so
overcome were simply 'unable to stand or sit' but had the
'use of their hands and can converse with perfect
composure'. In some cases, however, they are 'unable to
speak, the pulse becomes weak, and they draw a difficult
breath about once a minute' and 'all signs of life forsake
them for nearly an hour'. But once recovered these same
people said they 'felt no bodily pain, that they had the
entire use of their reason' and could 'relate everything that
had been said or done near them, or which could possibly
fall within their observation'.

One participant in the Cane Ridge revival remarked
that, having no invitation to preach on the Sunday, he
decided to preach anyway by using the 'body of a fallen
tree' to stand on.

I commenced reading a hymn with an audible voice,
and by the time we concluded singing and praying we
had around us, standing on their feet, by fair calculation
10,000 people. I gave out my text . . . 'For we must all
stand before the judgment seat of Christ' and before I
concluded my voice was not to be heard for the groans of
the distressed and the shouts of triumph. Hundreds fell
prostrate to the ground, and the work of conversion
continued on that spot until Wednesday afternoon. It
was estimated by some that not less than 500 were at one
time lying on the ground in deepest agonies of distress,

and every few minutes rising in shouts of triumph.

There seems to be some confusion which came first, the camp meeting or the revival. It seems probable that a work of the Spirit was abroad in Ohio, Kentucky, Tennessee, North Carolina and Virginia from 1790 onwards which in turn precipitated the desire to meet in a manner that became camp meetings. Many sometimes camped in tents near each other so they could have the benefit of the fellowship and worship. One historian has called the era from 1790 to 1810 America's 'second Great Awakening'. It crossed denominational lines although it would seem that it originally involved mostly Presbyterians and Methodists.

What was also reported was that at the height of the revival theological differences seemed to be in abeyance. One person, writing in 1802, stated that the Presbyterians 'appeared to have forgotten that they had any Confession of Faith or discipline, and the Methodists laid aside their Discipline, and seemed to forget that they were bound to observe rules contained therein'. However, one Presbyterian minister observed that

> the people among whom the revival began, were generally Calvinists; and although they had been long praying in words for the out-pouring of the Spirit... yet, when it came to pass that their prayers were answered, and the spirit [sic] became to flow like many waters... they rose up and quarrelled with the work, because... the subjects of it were not willing to adopt their soul-stupefying creed... the love of a saviour constrained them to testify, that one had died for all... but everything appeared new, and to claim no relation to the old bed of sand.

The same minister none the less years later signed his name to a doctrinal covenant that bound him to uphold the Confession of Faith. This suggests that the distance in time from the height of the revival sharpened doctrinal differences.

At the first camp meeting in 1799 an 'altar' was erected 'unto the Lord in the forest'. This would indicate that the practice of seeking the Lord by coming to an 'altar' was going on before 1799 – most probably by Methodists. One gave this description:

> It was in this great revival that camp meetings originated ... The grounds were generally laid out near to some flowing spring... a shelter in the centre for public worship... In front of the pulpit was the altar: this was designed as a place for penitents, where they might be collected together for prayer and religious instruction. This altar was usually made of poles, or square pieces of hewed timber placed on posts, at the four corners, with openings for ingress and egress. Inside the altar were seats, called by many, and sometimes in derision, the 'Mourner's bench'. At the close of the sermon or exhortation, an invitation was given for mourners, or penitents, to come to the altar – that is, such as were convinced of sin, and were inquiring 'what they should do to be saved', and were invited to approach seats set apart for them.

After the 'second Great Awakening' subsided, the Methodists kept up the practice of the altar or mourner's bench. The Presbyterians largely avoided this practice. Baptists tended to be divided on this issue; those who were more Calvinistic were less inclined to this practice.

The years 1810 to 1825 have been called the 'second phase of the second Great Awakening'. This was in many ways an era of moderate Calvinism, that is, a rigid Calvinism was opposed by men such as Timothy Dwight and Lyman Beecher. In the 1820s the rising star on the horizon was Asahel Nettleton, a man who was widely used in great revival. But soon another powerful preacher began to emerge on the American scene, and Nettleton's fame was partially eclipsed. For the dominant figure from 1824 to 1875 was Charles G. Finney, a Presbyterian.

While the use of the altar and mourner's bench became common in American Methodism, and not very much anywhere else, Charles Finney made this practice an integral part of his ministry. Finney introduced the anxious seat and the anxious meeting. As I said earlier, Charles Wesley might have used the former phrase. But the phrase itself gained currency with Finney. Finney described the anxious seat as 'the appointment of some particular seat in the place of meeting [usually the front benches or pews] where the anxious may come and be addressed particularly and be made the subject of prayers and sometimes conversed with individually'. He also felt that the anxious seat helped break the 'chains of pride'. The anxious meeting was held outside the place of meeting – possibly the basement of the church, the minister's house or a private home. The purpose of the anxious meeting was for more prolonged conversations with those who had not been convinced while sitting in the anxious seat.

Finney believed that the anxious bench constituted the use of means. Those who were willing to seek the Lord by sitting in this conspicuous place indicated an earnestness and willingness to follow the Lord. But in addition to the anxious seat Finney set up special inquiry rooms, located in the building, where the anxious or awakened could be taken. Finney wrote in his *Memoirs:* 'In this way conversion of a great many souls were secured'. But the main feature was the anxious seat – a visible place in the meeting for all to see. Finney even asked *church members* to come forward to the anxious seat and make professions of faith!

One reason for Finney's use of the anxious seat was that he felt that baptism had lost its meaning. This is why he even urged church members to come forward. He felt that many of these, though baptised, were still unconverted. Finney thus compared the anxious seat to the rite of baptism. Finney seemed not to realise that the anxious seat too might become a superficial ritual in the end.

Finney also advocated the use of protracted meetings,

not merely meeting on Sundays or mid-week. It would appear that after 1835 the term 'revival' was uncritically applied to such efforts. Some Calvinists objected to the fact that the anxious seat became an integral part of the protracted meetings. They felt that the anxious seat was a contrived means and felt that it militated against sound theology.

In some ways the nineteenth century was a repeat of the eighteenth century. In the eighteenth century there was the Arminian John Wesley and the Calvinist George Whitefield. In the nineteenth century there was Charles Finney (someone described his position as 'Arminianised Calvinism') and Asahel Nettleton. In the twentieth century there are those who want to line up behind either Whitefield or Wesley, and either Nettleton or Finney. Historians are anxious to vindicate their heroes and make claims to show which one God used the most! The truth is, God used *all* of these men. And if the lesson of the Cane Ridge revival of 1800 teaches us anything, the more the Spirit is present in power, the less defensive and divisive we become over our peculiar theological views.

As Charles Finney's days were coming to an end, still another important preacher came into prominence – Dwight L. Moody. He was the leading evangelical light during the last quarter of the nineteenth century. If Finney popularised the anxious seat, D. L. Moody popularised the inquiry room. Moody did not use the anxious seat, although he did have 'after meetings'. Moody wanted in fact to abandon the anxious seat, having grown up hearing unusual stories about emotionalism in the days of revival. He wanted little of this. A Boston reporter once said of Moody's meetings: 'No unconverted individual need hesitate to attend Moody's meetings for fear of being made conspicuous or uncomfortable'.

On the other hand, Moody did make very strong appeals to the unconverted. He asked those who were anxious to *stand* – not to sit in an anxious seat but to stand up before everybody and then make their way to the inquiry room. 'If a man is to be saved, he must take up his cross, and it is sometimes a great cross for a person to confess his anxiety before others. Many are blessed in the very act of rising,' Moody would say. But Moody was very determined that little emotion should be manifest. If one broke out with too many 'Amens' or 'Hallelujahs', Moody would stop in his sermon and say, 'Never mind, my friend, I can do all the hollering.' If a person persisted, Moody would ask the audience to sing a hymn while the usher removed the disturber. The man who was almost as well known as Moody, his song leader Ira Sankey, once said: 'We distinctly discountenanced any hysterical excitement, confusion, or noise.'

One historian observed: 'The days were long gone when Baptists and Methodists, let alone Congregationalists, Presbyterians and Episcopalians considered hysteria a manifestation of the Spirit and a certain sign of conversion.' If someone in his audience fainted, Moody would say calmly, 'Someone has fainted, but it is nothing. In large congregations like these it would not be strange to have four or five faint at each service. It is nothing remarkable. Satan wants to attract your attention in this way. But now never mind; let us go on with our attention on the sermon.'

Moody was adamant however that a man must confess Christ openly. Although he advocated the privacy of the inquiry room, the individual must take a stand before he entered such a room. 'The act of coming forward might require some effort, might even be embarrassing,' Moody would say, but he was fearful of emotionalism, and it was the inquiry room that he championed. 'In my own experience I find that where one person has been converted under the sermon, a hundred have been converted in the inquiry room.' Moody felt that this was largely because the people did not understand the theology of conversion.

In 1873 Moody sailed to Britain. This was in fact his third visit to the British Isles. He spent two years in Britain. Moody and Sankey spent four months in London. It is estimated that during these two years the total attendance at their meetings reached more than 2,500,000.

Moody gave his 'appeal' in Britain as he had done in the States.

Charles H. Spurgeon invited Moody to preach at the Metropolitan Tabernacle. Mr Moody particularly addressed the young men who were students at Mr Spurgeon's college. He said: 'I wonder how many of you would rise if I should ask every man and woman to do so who is ready to go and speak to some anxious soul – I wonder how many would rise and say, "I am ready, for one"?' The students and ministers at once rose in a body, and their example was quickly followed by members throughout the congregation. Then Moody said, 'Well, now you have risen, I want to tell you that the Lord is ready to send you. Nothing will wake up London quicker than to have the Christians going out and speaking to the people. The time has come when it should be done. We have been on the defensive too long.'

Spurgeon did not carry on the practice of making appeals at the Tabernacle. But he often urged awakened sinners to 'go below' (to the lecture hall) immediately after he preached. There the elders would counsel these souls and they would be interviewed by Spurgeon himself the next day if indeed they seemed to be converted. Spurgeon was not opposed to making an appeal. Dr Eric Hayden, formerly minister of the Metropolitan Tabernacle, insists that the Tabernacle was architecturally unsuitable for people to walk to the front and that this is why Spurgeon did not do it there. The proof that Spurgeon was not opposed to the practice, apart from the fact that he invited Moody into his pulpit, is that many of Spurgeon's own evangelists carried on this procedure all over London. A report in Spurgeon's magazine, *Sword and Trowel*, describes the results of one of his evangelists as follows: 'About a score came into the inquiry room nightly; and on Monday evening above fifty stood up to acknowledge having received Christ during the meeting, and another fifty to confess anxiety about their souls. I have the names and addresses of over a hundred who voluntarily sought help, and will welcome further care.'

Another report in the *Sword and Trowel* records a meeting which Spurgeon himself held at Providence Chapel, Shoreditch:

C. H. Spurgeon earnestly exhorted those who had accepted Christ as their Saviour to come forward amongst his people and avow their attachment to his person and name. Words of kindly encouragement and of loving persuasiveness, were addressed to the timid and retiring ones, who feared to avow themselves to be the Lord's, lest they should fall back into sin and dishonour his name. This was followed by an appeal to those who had confessed the name of Jesus – an appeal of so stirring and searching a nature, that many must have felt constrained to say, 'Lord what wilt thou have me to do?'

Spurgeon himself was converted in a Methodist chapel. He became a Calvinist, but he never forgot his roots. Nobody ever called Spurgeon a hyper-Calvinist.* The Arminians called him a Calvinist and the hyper-Calvinists called him an Arminian – a fairly good reputation! The rigid Calvinists were always suspicious of him and were never quite convinced he really was a Calvinist! Spurgeon was not in a theological strait-jacket. He even prayed once, 'Lord, send in all Thine elect, and then elect some more.'

Methodism in America took on a different shape and style from what had been known in England. I refer mainly to the camp meeting atmosphere and the practice of going out to the altar to seek the Lord. But there was another element that was introduced in Methodism: people began seeking sanctification* as much as justification – at the altar. What the seekers wanted was the immediate witness of the Spirit – to both. By the early nineteenth century Wesley's doctrine of sanctification was more and more systematised and the idea of 'two works of

*See appendix I

grace' became standard theological jargon in what became known as the Holiness Movement. People sought both to be 'saved' and also 'sanctified wholly'.

But this emerged also in England, partly through the influence of William Bramwell. As Wesleyan teaching became more and more systematised and the American influence found its way into Britain, the practice of going out to the front of the church – and kneeling – became common in a few churches. The emergence of the Salvation Army also saw the practice of going forward to pray, thus by the twentieth century 'appeals' in England were not altogether unknown. Between the influence of D. L. Moody and the revivalism of the Salvation Army the practice of going out to the front was somewhat established, although the percentage of churches that actually did this regularly was extremely small. In America the practice of going forward became very common among Baptists and holiness churches in the twentieth century, and some Baptists and holiness churches have carried this out in Britain as well.

Evangelist Billy Sunday possibly did more to cheapen the practice of going out to the front than any well-known figure of the twentieth century. He had been a famous baseball player and had also been converted from a life of drunkenness. He sometimes tended to equate being saved with dropping 'booze', although he no doubt led some people to the Lord who had no drink problem. But the thrust of his message was to 'hit the sawdust trail', which meant walking to the front of his tabernacle down the aisles that were covered with sawdust. He not only did away with the anxious seat but the inquiry room as well. His wife said that the inquiry rooms were not needed in Billy Sunday's ministry because he made the gospel so simple. Eternal life was received simply by shaking Billy Sunday's hand and signing a card. The penitent was handed a booklet which stated, 'By this act of coming forward... you are NOW the child of God' and 'you NOW have eternal life'.

'Do you believe it's right and manly to become a

Christian?' Billy Sunday would ask. 'Then come on down. If you don't, stay where you are.' Sometimes he would say, 'I want the inspiration of taking the hand of every fellow who says, "I'm with you for Jesus Christ and truth." Come on. You've been mighty fine tonight.' Sometimes he would say, 'Come on down and take my hand against booze, for Jesus Christ, for your flag.'

Billy Sunday's influence served to confirm to some people that there ought to be more to coming forward than merely shaking the preacher's hand and signing a card. The phrase 'praying through' became a cliché in some circles. One came to the front and knelt in order to 'pray through', that is, they wouldn't get up from their knees until they *felt* something happen inside themselves. They wanted a feeling that God had received them.

When Billy Graham first became popular on the American scene, he was often compared to Billy Sunday, partly because of his name and mostly because Billy Sunday was then a fairly well-known name in America. But Graham always wished to be identified with D. L. Moody. D. L. Moody was Graham's mentor, if anyone, and he largely dismissed any similarity between himself and Sunday. Indeed, Billy Graham's method is quite like that of D. L. Moody, not to mention his message.

This brief history should serve as a background to what I hope to unveil in this book. Church history is often called the laboratory for theology. We learn from the past. Billy Sunday was a long way from the Cane Ridge revival. But the Cane Ridge revival in my view was genuine. Much wildfire and fanaticism also emerged soon after the Cane Ridge revival. It always does, just as the practice of going forward can be cheapened. But somewhere in between there is a valid practice for non-revival times, a practice that is neither manipulative nor claiming to be the product of a heaven-sent revival.

This is why I put forward the public pledge. It is the biblical precedent that we must live up to and by this we may be sure we are honouring our Lord Jesus Christ.

3

CONSIDERING SOME OBJECTIONS

Not all who are a part of the Church today are very keen that men should be called immediately to confess Jesus Christ publicly. This is why I have felt moved to write this book. Having written a little book on tithing, I could not help but be interested to note the similarity that often exists between opposition to tithing and opposition to calling people forward to confess Christ. Opposition to either often arises out of the same milieu. There are of course exceptions. But it is none the less striking how similar the atmosphere is and how overlapping the arguments are with regard to the subject of tithing and that of calling people forward.

Let me give two examples. First, some want to say that there is no clear mandate in the New Testament to call for immediate decision and ask people to come forward to confess Christ publicly. These people want you to quote chapter and verse to prove from the Bible that this is what the minister or evangelist is required to do. If you cannot quote chapter and verse, they say, stop supporting this practice of calling people forward. The objection to tithing is essentially the same. Second, they want to show that the practice of calling people forward is a late innovation in church history. They are quite pleased to claim that great ministers like George Whitefield, John Wesley and Jonathan Edwards did not call people forward to confess Christ at the end of their sermons. Neither was tithing emphasised until recent times, say these people. It is therefore argued that one should rightly be suspicious of what does not have either antiquity on its side or the precedent of great men who were undoubtedly owned of God.

I hope I will be forgiven for being amused that most churches at the present time do not think much about stewards taking several minutes out of the service to take up a collection. I wonder where they get a chapter and verse out of the Bible for that? But I think I know why they do it.

However, my own call for this practice of a public pledge is based not on whether it works but whether it is biblical. That is *all* that really matters. I have asked myself whether there is more support for what I call public pledge than there is for tithing – or vice versa. I do not find more biblical support for one practice than the other. I would as readily defend one as the other. I also believe that both are equally needed today and I would predict that the church that practises both will be thriving and making an impact upon the world.

If one thinks at this stage that objections to calling for an immediate decision to confess Christ publicly only come from high Calvinist quarters, nothing could be further from the truth. I fear that Christianity today on both sides of the Atlantic is dominated by theological liberals who do not believe in heaven, hell, the deity of Jesus Christ and the need for conversion. I wonder what the state of Christianity would be today if all churches had stressed tithing and evangelism twenty years ago. But leaving tithing to one side, what a sight it would be if all churches today gave every visitor an opportunity to confess Jesus Christ publicly before he left the service! I do believe that if this practice were to begin everywhere now, there would be much greater hope for the Church in the world today and tomorrow.

In this chapter I want to consider fairly and carefully why it is that some would not be in favour of the public pledge taking place in every evangelistic service. To be sure, I am partly projecting; I therefore am partly referring to objections some have had to the traditional appeal, not to the practice I envisage (although the similarity is not to be entirely denied).

1.*Theological reasons.* The underlying explanation for most churches not engaging in the practice of calling people forward to confess Christ is theological. It may not always be consciously theological. Take, for example, the 4,151 Roman Catholic churches in Britain (figures based upon 1980 statistics). I have not heard of a Roman Catholic church that engages in the practice of calling people forward to confess Christ. For all I know, there are exceptions. But I suspect that it is something that is not done and I equally suspect that the reason for not doing it could be traced to their doctrine of salvation. They believe that one is regenerated through baptism. Therefore the absence of the practice of calling people forward to confess Christ as Lord and Saviour after a sermon in a Roman Catholic church has a theological explanation.

In 1980 there were 47,244 Protestant churches in the United Kingdom (including Greek Orthodox and Seventh-day Adventist). These include nearly 17,000 Churches of England, 8,000 Methodist churches, 3,500 Baptist churches, 6,700 Presbyterian churches and over 5,000 independent churches (such as Brethren, Congregationalists and Fellowship of Independent Evangelical Churches). Without intending to be judgmental but only objective, it would appear that over half of the Protestant churches in Britain disdain the idea of the public pledge because of their theological liberalism. One would not expect a minister to call people forward to confess Christ as Lord and Saviour if he does not believe in heaven, hell, the deity of Christ and the need for conversion. In other words, one's theological position precludes the very possibility of considering such a matter. Such a position is sometimes called universalist, the belief that everybody will ultimately be saved.

There is more than one kind of universalist, however. There is the theological liberal who does not believe God

would let anybody perish eternally. A person who believes
that is unlikely to feel a very great need to call men to
confess Christ publicly lest Christ deny him (cf. Matt.
10:33). There is also the universalist who believes that all
will be saved because Christ died absolutely and savingly
for all men. Some of Karl Barth's admirers may not
appreciate their position being described precisely in this
way, but it is not too surprising that this kind of thinking
has not sent very many missionaries into the world.
Conversion does not actually change one's final destiny
according to this view, therefore the need to confess Christ
openly is nipped in the bud by one's doctrine of
atonement.

The high Calvinist* actually has a similar doctrine of
atonement to that of Karl Barth, although the atonement
for the high Calvinist is limited to the elect. Thus Christ
died effectually for the elect alone and those for whom
Christ died will be saved sooner or later. The motivation to
call for conversions is often diminished by this theology,
although it must be said that (1) there are high Calvinists
who have a great evangelistic zeal and (2) there are
Arminians who have little burden for the lost. But I think I
can safely say that the high Calvinist opposes the
traditional practice of making an appeal for theological
reasons. I refer to the high Calvinist in that way to
distinguish him from the milder form of Calvinism which
I myself espouse. I do not believe that the Bible supports
the Puritan doctrine of limited atonement and I have
sought to show elsewhere (*Calvin and English Calvinism
to 1649*, Oxford) that Calvin himself did not teach it. I
therefore think that proponents of limited atonement
could be accurately called high Calvinists. Some would
even call them hyper-Calvinists.*

Because conversion is indeed the sovereign work of the
Holy Spirit, there have been those who fear that the call for
public decisions either (1) competes with the Spirit's own
work or (2) encourages decisions not induced by the Holy

*see appendix I

Spirit. I could not deny this possibility and I have some sympathy with this concern. The Rev. Iain Murray, in his booklet 'The Invitation System', summarises his position on this as follows: 'Our charge is that the invitation system leads inevitably to the danger of hastening unregenerate men to confess their "faith".' Mr Murray links this concern with the theological premise that 'only those who are predestinated' receive the call of the Holy Spirit and that the 'invitation system' has 'no connection with rebirth. Some are converted in spite of it, and not because of it.'

I agree that those 'ordained to eternal life' will believe (Acts 13:48) and that only those effectively called will be justified (Rom. 8:30). I don't agree that it follows that some are converted 'in spite' of being called to confess their faith publicly. The same God who predestines the end also predestines the means. I have no doubt that a minister's call for an immediate, public decision can be the very means of a person's genuine conversion. To dismiss the whole thing and say it is 'in spite' of a person walking to the front is like saying that the woman who was healed by touching the hem of Jesus' garment was healed in spite of the fact she touched the hem of His garment. After all, it was her faith that did it. But she *thought* she would be healed by touching Jesus' clothes. The incident was important enough to be recorded in God's word. It was a precious moment. I fear that the doctrine of predestination has led some to a fatalistic outlook on life. Some could, if not careful, leave half of living out because they dismiss the lovely ways in which God works. After all, it might also be said that if the aforementioned woman was predestined to be healed she would be healed anyway. Truly, I doubt that the Bible encourages us to think along such lines.

2. *Pragmatic reasons.* I believe there are a vast number of ministers who have no theological objections to making an appeal, but who believe that it is only productive under special circumstances. I now refer to Christians with solid,

evangelical views. I asked a fairly well-known clergyman if he ever made an appeal in his church. He did not, but said that he did so in a special mission. I asked, 'Why didn't you do it in your own church?' 'I don't know', he said, but supposed it was 'being uncertain how the congregation would cope'.

As I have indicated, one purpose of this book is to encourage the opportunity for a public pledge right in the church during a regular service, not just when there is a special mission. I do believe indeed that the special mission ought to be a regular feature of the Church's life. It would encourage more conversions. If one takes a non-Christian friend to hear Billy Graham, it is expected that the invitation to confess Christ publicly will come at the close of the sermon. Nothing is more thrilling than to have that non-Christian friend show an interest in the sermon and then actually walk out to the front. Such an expectation ought to characterise churches all the time!

If one can support Billy Graham's meetings, why not support his approach in churches everywhere? Most would be disappointed if the opportunity to walk forward was not given when Billy Graham preached. But Christians are not so disappointed when it does not happen in their own church, and I think they should be!

'It won't work', someone insists. To me this can be a vote of no confidence in the Holy Spirit. If we do believe that conversion is the sovereign work of the Holy Spirit, we ought equally to believe that a person truly converted will welcome the opportunity to confess his faith openly by walking to the front.

But someone will say that people are 'conditioned' for the invitation at the end of Billy Graham's sermon and therefore don't mind it. I am sure this is true. But why cannot this conditioning take place in every church? An atmosphere ought to be charged so that the very awareness of the opportunity to respond publicly to the sermon will make the non-Christian conscious of his position before God and the state of his own soul. I should think there is no healthier church on earth than the one which the non-

Christian is afraid to enter lest he be converted!

Some churches have some sort of an appeal when there is a baptismal service. I am glad about this. But why then? What if a baptismal service only comes a very few times a year? What about the time in between? Some ministers will call for people to respond publicly when they preach in the open air. Why only then?

If we really do believe that people dying without the Lord Jesus Christ as their Saviour are eternally lost, then it should sober us and make us think more seriously about inviting people to Christ and calling for decisions to confess Him. One should not wait for a special mission, a baptismal service or a Billy Graham crusade. Surely evangelism is the responsibility of the Church, and the regular preaching of the gospel to the non-Christian – with the call to confess Him now – should characterise every church under heaven. At the end of the day whether or not it works ought not to enter our minds. It just might be that this pragmatic principle at bottom is unconsciously theological – that either we do not really believe in the work of the Spirit or we don't believe that men dying without Christ perish forever in God's hell. Or perhaps we are more fatalistic than we realised?

3. *Cultural reasons.* A common observation about people walking forward to confess the Lord is that it is an American innovation and that it is all right to do it over there but not in Britain. I understand what people mean by this, but why is it that some British preachers or missionaries will go to foreign lands – like Africa – and call people to confess Christ publicly without blushing – but won't do it on British soil? It is not something that is done only in America.

One night after a difficult evening in Westminster Chapel I came to the vestry tired and distraught. Whereas I thought I had preached all right, not a single person walked forward. A dear friend of mine came in to see me. He didn't want me to feel bad because nobody came forward. Meaning to encourage me he said, 'I'm afraid you just won't get a Britisher to do that.' I looked at him and said, 'That then is why it is right to do this. If something is contrary to one's culture, personality and temperament, then it suggests that *only* the Holy Spirit can bring them to the front.'

The stigma of doing such a thing in Britain is very real. Charles Finney emphasised the anxious seat in America because baptism had lost its stigma. He therefore felt there was a need to bring back a stigma so that a certain amount of courage was required. I suggest that we are much like that in Britain. I have now lived in England for nearly eleven years. I grant that the culture is different. George Bernard Shaw said that America and Britain are 'separated by a common language'! The last thing in the world I have sought to do in my present church is to 'Americanise' it in the slightest bit. But the practice of calling men and women to confess Christ publicly ought to transcend culture.

In my book on tithing I said that Britishers have an opportunity to show their love for Christ in a way that an American might not. In America one can deduct the amount of money one gives to the Church from one's income tax and therefore be motivated to give to the Lord for less than pious reasons. But in Britain this is not possible. Thus to tithe in Britain and get no tax relief requires a tremendous devotion to the Lord indeed. I am essentially saying this again with regard to the public pledge. It is not common over here. It is not done very often. It therefore takes a great deal of courage. Thus when a person *does* move to the nearest aisle and walk to the front, often shaking like a leaf, it suggests the power of the Holy Spirit at work.

4. *Fear of man*. I am most sympathetic here. It may be that the fear of man is a chief reason why one does not call for an immediate commitment to confess Christ and follow Him. Speaking personally, the fear of failure was what I had to overcome. When the minister invites people to come to the front and confess their faith in Jesus, all eyes

are on that minister's face – and he knows it. For the very thought that nobody will respond is terrifying, especially if there are seasoned Christians out there in the congregation that are against the whole thing in the first place. It is an awful feeling when you know that there are actually people in the congregation who hope that nobody will go forward. I hope that the minister who may read this book never has to experience that.

But the fear of failure is enormous in any case. For the minister also knows how disappointed his supporters will be if nobody responds. They also fear failure for their minister's sake, for they do not want him to get discouraged if nobody comes. Thus all eyes are on the minister – both regular members and visitors. But when someone breaks the ice and moves to the front, all eyes move away from the minister – and the feeling is one of relief! (Unless it is a person who has done this before and someone that everybody knows – then all eyes turn to the minister again!)

The remedy for the fear of failure is assurance in the heart that it is the right thing to do. When you know this, you're set. When you are in doubt, your state of mind will fluctuate according to the response of the people in your services.

I should like to think that this book will encourage all who read it to know that it is simply the right thing to do. I do not say that lack of response will not be disappointing. There will be keen disappointments but never a feeling of being demoralised – when in your heart you have come to terms with this matter. Jesus asked, 'How can ye believe, which receive honour one of another, and seek not the honour that cometh from God only?' (John 5:44). That is the biblical principle that must be followed.

The fear of criticism cannot be underestimated. If a minister should begin to do this in his church, he will receive criticism from some. Perhaps not for theological reasons (as I had to face) but for reasons of breaking tradition (which I also had to face). Anytime we break tradition we will be in trouble with some. Moreover, all of us find it easier to do what is commonly done. That way nobody notices. But when one breaks tradition, it seems assertive. Most of us are afraid of appearing assertive.

There is also fear of ineptness, that is, of not carrying out the opportunity for a public pledge in the best possible manner. There is an art to this, as there is to preaching. I am still trying to improve my preaching and I am still trying to improve my way of inviting people to come to the front to confess their faith. Many times I have felt awkward in the way I handled giving the invitation and had a happy response, and other times I felt I handled it well and nobody came! This takes time and a little experience. But it will come and one ought to begin – like learning to swim.

But the greatest fear of all to overcome is simply that of offending the very person you are asking to come forward and confess the Lord – that one who, until now, has not been a Christian. In other words, it takes not a little courage to confront the sinner and tell him that he himself must receive the Lord now, confess Him now and stand up and be counted – now. For those who have learned to present the gospel on a one-to-one basis, the greatest fear to overcome is directly to invite that person to receive the gift of eternal life – now. And yet once a person has taken the step, it becomes not only something that seems natural but is something very desirable.

One of the reasons we have a natural fear of asking people to receive the Lord now and openly confess Him is that it appears to invade privacy. There is a strong feeling, both in Britain and in America, that religion is a 'private matter'. There is that old saying that the two things you don't discuss with people are religion and politics. For this reason there is a feeling in all of us that what we believe about religion and politics is nobody's business but our own. This is true in one sense; I have a right to my own opinion about religion and politics and it is nobody's business what I think. But we carry that idea too far, especially when we know that the only way another person can be saved is through hearing the gospel. We know that people are lost, going to hell and are in need of the gospel. We cannot sit still. We cannot keep quiet. God has committed unto us the ministry of reconciliation, as Paul said, 'We implore you on Christ's behalf: Be reconciled to God' (2 Cor. 5: 20, NIV). To keep quiet on this is to sin against Christ.

But surely the pulpit ought to be a recognised place from which confrontation with the gospel comes. It ought to be an accepted thing that the man in the pulpit is going to invite people to Christ. The person who may not have been in an atmosphere where the call for a public pledge is commonly done could be offended – at first. But the offence should not be taken too seriously. It may be that very confrontation which will bring home one's need to be saved in a manner that the preaching itself failed to do. I have observed this quite a number of times. I have enjoyed the irony of seeing more people coming into the vestry of Westminster Chapel since I have been calling people to the front who *didn't* go forward than before I began the practice. This was one thing that confirmed the validity of doing this. I can safely say that I have had more people seeking the Lord in my vestry in the past year who *didn't* walk forward than in the previous six years combined. It is now a common experience to have a person come in to see me after a Sunday evening service saying, 'I didn't go forward tonight. But I want to know how to become a Christian.' One example was a lady who came in weeping with this statement, 'I am so ashamed that I didn't have the courage to go forward. Is there any hope for me?' I assured her that there was indeed. I went over the gospel with her. She prayed to receive Christ. The following Sunday evening she came forward – during the first line of the first verse of the hymn. She was beaming with joy. She had looked forward to that all week. She also revealed to me that she had been coming to Westminster Chapel for three years but did not feel any urgency to think about her own soul until I began calling people forward.

The fear of offending people over invasion of privacy is largely the ploy of the devil to intimidate us – lest we get too zealous in our evangelism. The devil hates evangelism.

He hates it with a passion greater than that of the most sophisticated or simple person we are likely to encounter. We must remember that the 'god of this world' has blinded the minds of those who don't believe (2 Cor. 4:4). Anything that will be the means of waking them up will be a threat to Satan. I am convinced that the devil doesn't like the idea of this public pledge. He will play on our fears – making us think that our fear is a godly caution. He will play on our pride – making us think it is piety. He will play on our sophistication – making us think it is wisdom. If people are offended by the invitation for them to confess Christ, nine times out of ten it will be because they were already offended at the very gospel itself. And we must never be surprised when they are offended over the gospel. The message of 'Christ crucified' is a 'stumbling block' (Gr. *skandalon* – a scandal, an offence – 1 Cor. 1:23). Any effort to water down the gospel only makes it harder for a person to be saved; any effort to be less bold in asking them to commit themselves to Christ reflects our own fear – and does them no favour. If people are offended by our gospel and don't come back to hear us again, where are we sending them? They were on their road to hell when they came to us; we have the only thing that will help them. As Arthur Blessitt has put it, 'Where are you going to run them off to – hell number two, hell number three?'

May I say that it is also here where being a Calvinist is no disadvantage. I know that I am not going to lead savingly to Christ one of the 'non-elect' (to use the term put to C. H. Spurgeon), neither can I dislodge any of God's chosen. But what I *can* do is to be God's catalyst to bring men to see their need of a Saviour.

We must ever keep in mind that this so-called 'right to privacy' will soon come to an end. Jesus said, 'Do not be afraid of them. There is nothing concealed that will not be disclosed, or hidden that will not be made known. What I tell you in the dark, speak in the daylight; what is whispered in your ear, proclaim from the housetops. Do not be afraid of those who kill the body but cannot kill the soul. Rather, be afraid of the one who can destroy both soul and body in hell' (Matt. 10:26-8, NIV). At the great judgment all people will surrender their 'right to privacy'. They will kiss it goodbye forever and ever. The call that confronts men now is nothing more than a taste of judgment in advance. It is a most kind invitation, a most kind warning. This is why Jesus went on to say, 'Whoever disowns me before men, I will disown him before my Father in heaven' (Matt. 10: 33, NIV).

Finally, there is in the end no good reason for the fear of failure. Why? Because only God can save. 'A man can receive only what is given him from heaven' (John 3: 27, NIV). 'No one can come to me unless the Father who sent me draws him' (John 6:44, NIV). 'The Spirit gives life; the flesh counts for nothing' (John 6:63, NIV). What is more, when people turn down my invitation, it is not me they are rejecting. They are rejecting Christ. God said to Ezekiel, 'When I say to a wicked man, "You will surely die", and you do not warn him or speak out to dissuade him from his evil ways in order to save his life, that wicked man will die for his sin, and I will hold you accountable for his blood. But if you do warn the wicked man and he does not turn from his wickedness or from his evil ways, he will die for his sin; but you have saved yourself' (Ezek. 3: 18-19, NIV). The public pledge is one way we may demonstrate how seriously we take these awesome verses, for they remind us that it is our duty to warn. The call to confess Christ immediately and publicly is not only a high privilege but contains an implicit warning.

4

THE PURPOSE OF THE PUBLIC PLEDGE

I have stressed a public confession of Christ rather than a public receiving of Christ with regard to the public pledge. This is because I see the public pledge as having an essential purpose; namely, confessing openly what is already true. I suspect that this is an aspect that has not always been emphasised in connection with the traditional appeal to come forward in a public meeting. The main thing to be said about confessing Christ is that it shows that one is not ashamed of Him. This is why it is done in public. This is also why Dr Billy Graham has stressed that when Christ called people to Himself, He did so publicly.

What must never be underestimated is that God is honoured when people confess Him openly. So many of the psalms are devoted to the praise of God. God inhabits the praises of men. When His name is praised, He delights in it. It ought not to be thought a surprising thing when He honours those who praise Him publicly. Those whom God has honoured most of all have been those who have been bold and open with their faith. Many have heard about Daniel being in the lions' den and how God shut the mouths of the lions when Daniel was thrown in with them. Less well known is why Daniel was thrown into the lions' den. It was not merely because Daniel trusted God but because he 'went public' with his faith. A decree was published that anybody who prayed to any god would be

thrown into the lions' den – a law that was passed in order
to expose Daniel. Daniel might have said to himself, 'I
don't have to let everybody know about my faith. Surely I
can believe in secret.' But no. When Daniel learned that
the decree had been published, 'he went home to his
upstairs room where the *windows opened* towards
Jerusalem. Three times a day he got down on his knees and
prayed, giving thanks to God, just as he had done before'
(Dan. 6:10, NIV). The thrust of the story of redemption in
the Bible from cover to cover is that those who believe in
God must not be ashamed of it.

I now wish to elaborate on the account of the woman
who touched the hem of Jesus' garment and was suddenly
healed. At the precise moment she touched Jesus' clothes,
our Lord felt 'virtue' go out of His body! The healing had
already taken place and Jesus knew it. The Lord might
merely have passively rejoiced that someone in the crowd
was healed. He might also have spared Himself one more
conversation. After all, a healing is a healing and this was
nothing new to Jesus. What is more, there were more
people who needed His help. But no, Jesus was not going
to let that little lady get away with a 'secret' deliverance!
He whirled around and asked, 'Who touched my clothes?'
This to the disciples was an inane question. 'You see the
people crowding against you', they answered, 'and yet you
can ask, "Who touched me?"' But Jesus kept looking
around to see who had done it. 'Then the woman,
knowing what had happened to her, came and fell at his
feet and, *trembling with fear*, told him the whole truth'
(Mark 5:25-33, NIV).

Jesus made her do it. But the healing had already taken
place. And yet there was something sealed in her coming
out of hiding, for Jesus said, 'Go in peace and be freed
from your suffering', as though the healing had not taken
place (Mark 5:34, NIV). There was something incomplete
even though power to heal had gone out of Jesus' body.
This matches all else the Bible says about the importance
of coming out of hiding.

The essential purpose of the public pledge is that men

should confess Christ, that is, share with everybody what has already taken place in the heart. It is indeed like the lady with the issue of blood who was healed but was none the less required to confess what had already happened to her. My conception of the public pledge is essentially this, confessing what is already true.

I would have thought that this magnifies the power of the gospel *alone* to save a person. God can save a man while he is seated in the pew of the church, or riding in a bus or train, or while he is walking in the park. Or at home. Regeneration in any case is an unconscious work of the Spirit. At what point an individual is actually regenerate it is virtually impossible to know. Those who claim they know the day and the hour when they were converted are more accurately describing the assurance of their salvation. Regeneration – that grace of God which enabled them to see the Lord's glory and power – took place before their conscious awareness of it, even if it was a second before!

The preaching of the gospel itself is the instrument of conversion. 'God was pleased through the foolishness of what was preached to save those who believe' (I Cor. 1:21, NIV). Paul said, 'I am not ashamed of the gospel, because it is the power of God for the salvation of everyone who believes' (Rom. 1:16, NIV). 'When you received the word of God, which you heard from us, you accepted it not as the word of men, but as it actually is, the word of God, which is at work in you who believe' (I Thess. 2:13, NIV). It was faith at work in the heart that made this possible.

A woman named Lydia heard Paul preach. It is said that 'the Lord opened her heart to respond to Paul's message' (Acts 16:14, NIV). Jesus said, 'For just as the Father raises the dead and gives them life, even so the Son gives life to whom he is pleased to give it' (John 5:21, NIV). This is done as people hear the word that is preached. Conversion is supernatural. It is miraculous – as miraculous as the healing of the woman with bleeding. For it is only the sovereign work of God that 'rescued us from the dominion of darkness and brought us into the kingdom of the Son he loves' (Col. 1:13, NIV).

Conversion, then, is in the heart. 'For it is with your heart that you believe and are justified' (Rom. 10:10, NIV). If it does not happen in the heart, a thousand confessions with the lips will be of no avail. You can walk forward every night in a Billy Graham campaign or every Sunday in a church service in which a public pledge is made available, but if the heart is not *opened*, the 'conversion' is like a vaccination that does not take.

The public pledge may be described as a preacher's inquiry whether or not there is one in the congregation who has believed. In other words, the conversion most likely took place either during the sermon or at some time prior to that particular moment. It is simply an invitation to come out of hiding, to 'go public' with your faith in Jesus.

When I come to the end of a sermon, I often put it like this. 'You have heard the gospel. Do you believe it? If so, are you ashamed of it? If you have believed this gospel and are not ashamed, show it by sharing it with us tonight.'

Many times I will close with what is often called 'the sinner's prayer', putting it something like this. 'If all that I have said in this sermon is still unclear to you, let me now make it as easy as possible for you. I want you, there in your seat, to pray a prayer in your heart. You need not say it out loud. God sees your heart. He knows whether you mean it. Even if you begin praying the prayer but find there is something you cannot say to God and mean, fine – stop praying. Only keep praying to God if you mean every word of it from your heart.' Then I will offer a prayer like this: 'Dear God, I know I am a sinner . . .' (I pause long enough for them to repeat this in their hearts). 'I am sorry for my sins . . . I confess my sins to you, some I remember, some I've forgotten . . . I believe that Jesus died for all of my sins . . . Wash away my sins by His precious blood . . . I welcome the Holy Spirit . . . As well as I can, I give you my life . . .' I then say to them, 'If you have prayed that prayer, I want you to share it with us. Jesus said, "If you confess me before men I will confess you before my Father". I am going to give you an opportunity to do precisely this in the next few moments. We are going to close this service with the singing of a hymn. During this hymn you may confess your faith by coming out to the front of the church. Make your way to the nearest aisle and walk to the front. Your doing this will send a signal to the world that you are not ashamed that you have received Jesus as your Saviour. When you come down here to the front, I will come and join you. I'm not going to ask you to make a speech or anything like that. Your very coming will be a way of confessing Christ openly.' Generally speaking, that is the way I do it.

Sometimes I will make an appeal to the backslider, especially if the sermon particularly lent itself to one who was saved long before but has been disobedient. One must be careful here. There will be those who have what the Puritans called an 'overly scrupulous conscience', and they may think that they too ought to come forward. When I first started doing this in Westminster, some of the same very sensitive Christians came forward every week or two – supposing that the act of coming forward would either be a quick cure for their backsliding (such as it was) or at least show God they wanted to please Him. As it turned out, none of these should have come forward and I told them so. They stopped. By backslider I mean one who has clearly gone back on his initial profession of faith; he has not been living for the Lord, has gone into deep sin or has been outside the church community for some time. When the preaching particularly affects a person like this, there is good reason to believe that he most certainly ought to reaffirm his commitment to Christ. Doing so publicly lets everybody know of his repentance and it also places him in the position of realising that others will be watching his life from now on with more interest and care. In other words, the public pledge can seal the backslider's return to the fold.

I think that most would agree that there is no human pressure in this approach. This does not mean that some will not criticise. I doubt that there is any kind of practice

along these lines that will be entirely free of criticism. I
might say moreover that it has been interesting to me that
a good many people (who heard rumours about what we
have been doing in Westminster) were pleasantly surprised when they saw for themselves what it was like.
'How can anybody criticise that?' they have said. At any
rate, what I have described is what I mainly mean by
public pledge; it is a call to people to share openly what
has already happened to them.

The instrumental purpose

Whereas the essential purpose of the public pledge is to
invite people to confess what has already happened to
them, there is inherent in this very approach another
reason for doing it. Some will no doubt say it should be the
main reason. I am not so sure that it is the main reason, as I
shall explain below. I now refer to what I would call the
instrumental purpose of the public pledge: it allows
people to seek the Lord in a public manner, although they
may not be sure they are saved.

The call to confess Christ publicly allows many people
to go forward who aren't sure why they are doing it but
somehow feel it is the right thing for them to do.
Sometimes a person who has walked to the front does not
know why he is there. It is not unusual if, when I ask a
person who has just moved out to the front, 'Why have you
come?' that he answers, 'I don't know'. There is nothing
wrong or suspicious about this. A person who has been
deeply affected by the preaching is often anxious to 'do
something' then and there to show (if only to show
himself) that he wants to go on with God and get his life
sorted out. A lot of good can follow this – not the least of
which is actual conversion. But if conversion has not
taken place as yet, it is still helpful for many people that
they have come forward. Why? Because (1) the gospel can
be further clarified to them by a counsellor or the minister
and (2) a fresh contact will have begun which allows for a
warm rapport with the minister or counsellor that

otherwise would not have been possible. Had the person not gone to the front, especially if he was one who does not often go to church, the possibility exists that nobody would have noticed this person's presence in the service, not to mention the possibility he might never come back to church again.

The person who has come forward but has not been converted will be made to see this by an experienced counsellor. Whenever a person walks to the front in Westminster Chapel I nod to particular people in the congregation who are qualified to talk with such people, and they take them to a separate room – the equivalent of the inquiry room of D. L. Moody's day. The first thing that a counsellor does is to inquire whether or not a person understands the basis of having eternal life. If the person has not been converted, he will soon see that going forward did not save him but it most certainly establishes a contact with a Christian who will try to be of help. Often, the person who has come forward will receive the gospel in the quietness of the separate room. The conversion therefore took place after he walked forward.

If it is discovered that the person who has walked to the front is truly converted and merely came out to the front to confess what was already true, a counsellor will rejoice with that person, take his name and address, then send him on his way with some good literature. I will say more about the role of a counsellor and the matter of follow-up below.

There are times when the Spirit of God is present in a service in great intensity and, when that happens (something rare nowadays, I fear), one should be thankful and seize upon that moment with all the earnestness possible. Sometimes the Spirit is present in intensity with *only one person* – even hidden from the minister. That person is gravely conscious that he or she has been personally confronted by the most high God. Such a person often comes to the front weeping. Extreme care is needed from one who understands both Holy Spirit conviction and also the gospel. Such a person can often be led to receive Christ after the service is finished.

A minister must be as sensitive as possible to the presence of the Spirit. I myself have a lot to learn about this. I think it is important to be flexible in calling people forward. The public pledge as I have outlined it is the safe thing to do – every time. But if the power of the Spirit was felt in an undoubted manner, one might go further. Admittedly great caution should be exercised here; for it is at this point that abuses could creep in (I shall come to them later) and Pandora's box could be opened for all sorts of things (not the least of which is the desire for numbers, etc.). But I am talking about the unusual sense of God's presence.

When the Spirit is present in power the minister should, in W. A. Criswell's phrase, 'draw in the net'. It is absolutely right to say, 'You know who you are and you ought to come tonight without delay.' The problem of course here is that you sometimes have those ministers who (1) feel they must pretend the Spirit is present in power all the time, (2) think they can 'work up' the Holy Spirit or (3), dare I say it, are high-pressure evangelists who are playing a game.

Let me give an example of what I mean by an intensity of the Holy Spirit's presence. In a previous church of which I was the pastor I noticed in the congregation a man for whom many had been praying to be saved. His wife was a member of the church, but he would not come with her to the services. I called on him at his home, presented the gospel to him and established a warm rapport; but he would not receive the Lord.

One Sunday evening in Fort Lauderdale, lo and behold, there he was in my service. It was the first time he had been in that church (to my knowledge). The Lord was present in the service in a powerful way. I had a good deal of liberty in preaching. The closing hymn was 'Just as I am without one plea'. I invited people to come forward to confess Christ. I saw him staring at the floor instead of singing as we went into the third verse of the hymn. As we sang the fourth verse I thought he was going to squeeze the top of the pew in front of him to shreds! He was seated right next to the centre aisle, about five rows back. I could see everything plainly. The blood vessels in his hands stood out as though one had put a tourniquet on his arm. Tears began to roll down his cheeks as we came to the fifth and final verse. The hymn ended and he stayed in place, standing as if immobilised. I knew he was in utter misery. I felt so sorry for him. I knew the Spirit of God was at work. Normally I did not do this but I broke my own rule – I decided to repeat the first verse. I was afraid the man would never come back again if I allowed him to go out of the door of the church. I announced that we would repeat the first verse of the hymn, for 'there might be somebody who is so miserable that he would be in worse shape if he left as he is'. That man – in answer to the prayers of many – took a step into that aisle, and literally staggered to the front, his shoulders shaking as he sobbed with each step. I walked down to meet him as he reached the front. He wept on my shoulders. At the same time another man came forward for whom many also had been praying.

Those were the only two that night – a night of nights in my ministry at that church. The second man became a deacon of that church, and the first man became the chairman of the pulpit committee to seek a new pastor after I had gone.

The instrumental purpose of the public pledge, then, is that it allows people to come forward who are *seeking* the Lord. People need not be addressed directly every time with 'You *must* come tonight or you may never have another chance.' But by faithfully presenting the opportunity of a public response those who aren't really ready to confess that anything *has* happened can none the less confess what they hope *will* happen. Should it 'happen' (real conversion, of course) after such a person has come out to the front, I do not see any need for the same person to go out to the front the following week. The signal he intended to send to the world that he is unashamed has already been sent. I see no need for a person to go forward twice unless the second time is a case of a returning backslider.

The very practice of the public pledge often releases the Spirit to work more deeply. Why? Because it is so easy to quench the Holy Spirit. When the Spirit is at work in the message but no opportunity for an open, public response is given, the Spirit will often be quenched by the sheer uninterest that usually comes after a person has gone back to the daily routine of life.

On the day of Pentecost men cried out, 'What shall we do?' If Peter had been like some of us, he would have said to them, 'Now, folks, don't get too excited. Relax. There's plenty of time. We wouldn't want you to do anything under pressure. You may be sorry tomorrow. If what you feel is real, you will feel the same in six months from now, and that is all that really matters. Go on home and think about what you have heard. God bless you. Amen.'

Hardly. Peter knew that these men who were cut to the heart wanted some release from their consternation. They were miserable. They were ready. Peter told them there *was* something they could do and that they could do it right away, 'Repent and be baptised, *every one of you*'. That wasn't enough. 'With many other words he warned them; and he *pleaded* with them, "Save yourselves from this corrupt generation"' (Acts 2:38, 40, NIV). As we know by now, 3,000 were added to their number the very same day. No delay. Peter wouldn't allow any delay. For when the Spirit is at hand in great power, one must take full advantage of it. The same outpouring may never return again. So by giving a regular, calm and clear opportunity for people to respond, two things are more possible as a consequence: (1) the minister himself may feel the liberty to press further than usual, and (2) there may be a movement of the Spirit on a person who at first seemed unlikely to be moved – not yet converted but seeking.

There is another aspect of the instrumental purpose, namely that conversion itself sometimes takes place at the moment one walks forward. It would be a mistake to overestimate this, as well as the number of times it actually occurs; but it would also be a mistake to underestimate it. As D. L. Moody put it, 'some are blessed in the very act of rising'. Indeed, it is not an uncommon occurrence for one literally to feel the witness of the Spirit that one is saved in the very act of moving to the front. I know a man who said to me, 'The moment I stepped into the aisle, I felt something happen in my heart'. He is the minister today of a church in Ohio. What this man felt was undoubtedly the witness of the Holy Spirit. Once a person becomes willing to follow the Lord, and proves his willingness by walking out to the front, it is not at all uncommon that the Holy Spirit testifies powerfully to such a person at that moment. This to me is another confirmation that God honours the practice of going out to the front. It has happened to thousands and I have no doubt that it is a practice that emerged in church history under the leadership of the Spirit.

But what I have been careful *not* to say is that the act of walking forward is *receiving* Christ. The primary purpose of the public pledge is to *confess* Christ; the instrumental purpose is to *seek* the Lord. But I am constrained to come short of saying that the decision to go forward is to *receive* Christ. Otherwise the act of walking to the front is no more than a Protestant sacrament. This was, I feel, Billy Sunday's error and it is, I fear, the error all too common in some places today. Whereas God often witnesses to the very one who makes the move to the front, it would be a great mistake to imply that walking down the aisle is receiving eternal life. Unless a person walks forward to confess Christ – going public with what has already happened – the value of going forward is *counselling*. The minister therefore must give his invitation with theological integrity. This is why I put the instrumental purpose subsidiary to the primary purpose.

And yet the very practice of going out to the front was born in revival which related almost entirely to what I have called the instrumental purpose. The reason Eleazar Wheelock called people to the front was that they might get help. So with the Cane Ridge revival. As far as I am able to tell, it was not a matter of people confessing Christ in revival times, they were seeking Him!

It will therefore be thought by some that what I call the instrumental purpose should really be the primary purpose of going forward – if only because the very practice was born in revival. But I think otherwise. We are not in revival at the moment. I think it is utter folly to pretend. There is no great conviction of the Spirit abroad that I can see, not many people asking, 'What must I do to be saved?' The reason there was a need for a mourner's bench was because the Spirit was present in power. People were literally mourning. They were weeping, crying, anxious, desperate and in agony. A mourner's bench was useful. But to keep up the mourner's bench because it was born in revival is like trying to imitate shaking, jerking, quaking, wailing and other hysterical manifestations which were not uncommon in those times of revival.

The public pledge safeguards theological integrity. To invert the order in non-revival times, it seems to me, borders on (1) competing with the Spirit's work and (2) looking for heads to count. But by making the essential, primary purpose that of confessing what is already true, the very opportunity of walking forward keeps the door open for those with whom the Spirit is undoubtedly at work. The very practice of going forward presses home the need to look at the state of one's soul. It also honours the biblical mandates to seek the Lord. 'Seek ye the Lord while he may be found, call ye upon him while he is near' (Isa. 55:6). The minister can say this faithfully every time he preaches. And should the Spirit of God be at work, how wonderful it is that the opportunity of the public pledge is given.

The call for public commitment gets its impetus not from church history but from Abraham's public pledge after he had been blessed by Melchisedek. That pledge is always in order. Abraham wanted to stand up and be counted. As Paul stressed how the gospel began with Abraham (Gal. 3:8), it should not be surprising that the best outline for a Christian confession of faith came also with Abraham.

So in summary, although the practice of going out to the front was born in revival, it does not follow that the practice itself is valid only in revival times. My solution is one that is honouring to God in non-revival times but allows the Spirit to work visibly with men in a way that might not be seen were the public pledge not made available. The public pledge simply allows people to respond immediately to what they have heard should God be powerfully at work. It is our desire that He should always be at work. Giving people the opportunity to confess Christ publicly discloses the minister's fervent wish that God will work powerfully every time he preaches. Making the public pledge available shows that the minister is motivated by a spirit of expectancy even in non-revival times.

Most of all, the public pledge allows men, women, teenagers, boys and girls to stand up and be counted in an age that is grim and bleak. What a contrast! I often say to my congregation after one or more have walked to the front of a Sunday evening, 'Where in London can you find a sight like this? People at this moment are drinking, lusting, looking for pleasure and fun; but what a beautiful sight this is!'

The spontaneity that gave birth to the practice of openly seeking the Lord also opened the way for men to confess the Lord's grace to them by showing they are not ashamed. Not all that happens in revival should be allowed to disappear simply because the spontaneity is gone. What often begins as spontaneous is to be continued by effort because it was right in the first place. The effort, however, is not on the part of those who stand up to be counted. The effort is on our part who will be willing to make the public pledge possible. It will be spontaneous for those who will stand up to be counted. It is to be carried out because we believe that the Holy Spirit is still at work in the 1980s – even if the extraordinary revival we pray for is delayed.

5

ABUSES

Everything I wish to uphold in this book is vulnerable to abuse. The people will not usually be the guilty ones. Yes, some will walk to the front hoping for a quick cure. Some will do it for attention. But the real culprit will almost always be the minister who, having opened the way for people to come forward, cannot bear the thought of nobody coming. It is pride that does it. Or fear of what people will say when there is no success.

It is often said that great revival breeds fanaticism and wild fire. Indeed, the Kentucky village of Shakertown is barely ten miles from where the Cane Ridge revival broke out in 1800. As the real revival resulted in people being struck down by God's power, so did Satan imitate God's work and turn his instruments' rods into serpents, (cf. Exod. 7:10ff). People around those parts took *shaking* as an infallible sign that God was at work.

Another counterfeit that outlived the revival was the manipulations of preachers and evangelists to get people out to the front. In the beginning the mourner's bench was needed. But as the revival began to wane, there were those who wouldn't admit that the revival was over. So they began to coax people to come to the mourner's bench and pray. Now and then, true, God blessed certain efforts along these lines. But the danger is obvious. The mourner's bench became a test to see whether God was at work and whether the preacher or evangelist really had the unction that would get people out to the front.

There are actually evangelists abroad at the present time who send letters to pastors and who guarantee 'so many professions'. One evangelist in America, for instance, advertises himself and guarantees a certain number of conversions to the pastor who will invite him.

The theology that lies behind the present book is one that appeals to the mind, heart and will – in that order. 'But God be thanked, that ye were the servants of sin, but ye have obeyed from the heart that form of doctrine which was delivered you' (Rom.6:17). Doctrine, or teaching, begins in the mind. It proceeds from the mind to the desire (the heart) and from there to voluntary decision (the will). But if a minister by-passes the mind and plays on the emotions and appeals directly to the will, he has departed from New Testament theology.

Sometimes 'heart' and 'mind' are used interchangeably in the Bible (cf. Heb. 8:10 and Heb. 10:16). Sometimes the 'heart' means one's affections (Eph. 6:6) and sometimes 'heart' means the will (Col. 3:22). But Paul's statement in Romans 6:17, because he mentions doctrine, shows that the obedience that God wants must begin in the mind. One must have a certain perception. The Spirit uses the word. That is Paul's argument in Romans 10:17. One must lay hold of certain things that are declared *about* God, Jesus Christ, sin, salvation before one can be saved. To appeal to the emotions of a person in order to secure some sort of response, when there has been no opportunity to grasp what truth is, does men no favour and can positively harm the honour of Christ.

But some of the best evangelists in history have fallen to the temptation to play on the emotions of people. There is a story concerning George Whitefield that many of his admirers would prefer to forget. Had Whitefield been an Arminian, you can be sure that some Calvinists of today would go for him tooth and nail as they do certain evangelists whose theology is suspect! George Whitefield asked a man who played a trumpet to play on signal at a particular point in his sermon. George Whitefield's point came as he was describing Gabriel blowing his trumpet, signifying that the second coming of Jesus had taken place. Using I Corinthians 15:52 ('at the last trump') and I Thessalonians 4:16 ('The Lord himself shall descend from heaven with a shout . . . and with the trump of God'), Whitefield had a secret arrangement with this trumpeter. On signal this man would start to play his trumpet – several hundred yards away, out of everyone's sight. Once the trumpeter got Whitefield's signal and began to play, Whitefield would look at the sky and shout, 'STOP! GABRIEL, STOP!' The trumpet continued. Whitefield cried to heaven, 'NO, GABRIEL. STOP PLAYING, THERE ARE PEOPLE HERE THAT AREN'T READY. STOP, GABRIEL, STOP!' By then the hysterical crowd began to cry out to God for salvation. This was not Whitefield's finest hour.

I would have thought that George Whitefield, often held up as one who never made an appeal, was the first example of abusing the principles that safeguard the theological integrity of the public pledge. But Whitefield was none the less a mighty man of God, probably the greatest evangelist since the Apostle Paul. Yet he was human and sometimes went too far. We must keep Mr Whitefield in mind as we examine abuses. For it is not only the Arminian, or Pelagian,* who abuses the practice of calling for public commitment.

With my own background as a resource, I think I could match any story I have ever come across in terms of abuses of the public invitation to confess or seek Christ. I am from Ashland, Kentucky, a town that is a good distance from Cane Ridge. And yet there was a revival spirit around in my part of Kentucky in the early part of this century. Some of it was genuine, some of it was counterfeit. One of the most popular preachers around as I was growing up was C. B. Fugett. After he retired, I got to know him quite well. We spent many hours together, often playing croquet and golf. He had had some genuine experiences of revival, one or two of which sound a lot like Cane Ridge. But he too fell

*See appendix I

prey at times to the temptation to play on people's emotions. In a manner reminiscent of Whitefield, my old friend C. B. Fugett on one occasion (I am assured he only did it once), preaching on 2 Peter 2:4 (the fallen angels being delivered 'into chains of darkness'), had all the lights of the church turned out at the climax of his sermon, then had somebody drag noisy chains across the front of the church which had the effect of making people think they were already in hell.

Evangelist Fugett has gone to be with the Lord since we have been living in England. It has been estimated by many that he led over 100,000 souls to Christ. He once told me of an occasion when he preached in a camp meeting with Seth Rees (father of Dr Paul Rees) when people were struck down by the power of God and would lie unconscious for an hour or more before waking up with a great assurance of sins forgiven. What I think should be learned from that is this. When God has acted in an extraordinary manner it is tempting to think that His power can be turned on or off at will. A person may begin to take things into his own hands before he realises it. This I suspect is the explanation for what happened in Whitefield's day and how Whitefield himself could at times go too far in trying to move people's wills. But a person should not be regarded as phoney simply because he has abused certain theological principles that are held dear.

The worst case of crowd manipulation I can recall was when a youthful evangelist came to my church in Ashland, Kentucky. On the final night of the revival he preached on 'the unpardonable sin' and the 'blasphemy of the Holy Ghost'. He told several moving stories of people who waited too long to become Christians and who died without Christ. I do not doubt that there was an awesome feeling of conviction in that packed church. After the sermon the evangelist had everybody stand. 'Everyone stand, please.' He waited until all were on their feet. Then he said this. 'If you know beyond a shadow of a doubt that you are ready to meet God were you to die at this moment, I will ask you to sit down.' As people began to sit he shouted, 'WAIT. DON'T SIT DOWN! Be absolutely sure. Do not lie to the Holy Ghost. Remember Ananias and Sapphira who were struck dead when they lied to the Holy Ghost. But if you are absolutely sure that you are ready to meet God, do sit down.' By then half the crowd was still standing. He then addressed them and urged that they come to the front to kneel for prayer before they went out of the church. About half of those standing did so. I suspect that this young evangelist was wanting a sensational stir on the last night of his stay at that church. He got it.

In chapter two I mentioned that in the nineteenth century there was as much seeking the Lord for sanctification as there was for justification; this occurred in the Holiness Movement. Parallel to Finney's call to church members to take their place in the anxious seat was the call for saved people to get 'sanctified wholly'.* Thus an evangelist's success was often measured merely by how many came to kneel. With entire sanctification (the way it was often preached) being out of reach of the most conscientious saints, evangelists had no difficulty in getting seekers to the front. Once the seeker came to the front to kneel, a counsellor would often ask, 'Do you want to get saved or do you want to get sanctified?' Whatever the answer, the formula was virtually the same: give your heart completely to God. One was not encouraged to leave the place of kneeling until one felt the witness that one was either saved or sanctified wholly. In some cases, when no witness of the Spirit came to the seeker, he would often be instructed to take his salvation (or equally his entire sanctification) by faith. 'Claim the promise' was often the counsel.

I cannot help but think that the time came when some evangelists did not care what happened to people after they came forward. It was their job to get the people out to the front, the counsellors' job to take it up from there. The evangelist's sole task was to move people – to get them to

*See appendix I

respond, stand, raise a hand, walk, run, skip, hop, jump – as long as there was a stir. It seems to me that it is no different from a high-pressure salesman who takes the order, gets the down-payment on the product, then goes his way rejoicing with his commission – not caring one whit whether the people like or intend to pay for what they bought.

In many Southern Baptist churches one can go forward for any number of reasons: to confess Christ, to seek the Lord, to join the church, to be baptised, to rededicate one's life, to declare oneself called to full-time Christian service and other reasons! The pressure is often on the minister to have some sort of response. The result is sheer bondage, one that many ministers would like to extricate themselves from but don't know how.

I know one man who admitted that he went forward at the age of seven because he was promised a silver dollar if he came to the front. He was then told that he was saved by coming forward and was taken right into membership of the church!

A close friend of mine who is a Southern Baptist pastor told me of a church leader who came to his congregation to preach on a special occasion. The guest preacher addressed the members of the church. He preached the kind of sermon that made the sincere Christian wonder if he had ever been truly converted. The consequence was that hundreds came to the front. This church leader was whisked off to his next assignment, only to do the same thing the following evening somewhere else. It seems that some ministers want nothing more than an immediate effect – any kind of stir. What happens later does not seem to matter. In the case just described, my pastor friend assures me it will not happen again, for that church leader will not be invited back. But some pastors are not so discerning. They seem only to want the superficial appearance of what could be taken by some as a mighty movement of the Spirit of God. But it is so often as phoney and as horrific as any episode of fanaticism that is distasteful.

Abuses come when the will or emotions are appealed to rather than the mind. What matters is doctrine – teaching that is clearly presented to the mind and understood. I am not saying that light comes before life (that is, knowledge before regeneration) because the mind must be quickened before what has been heard can be grasped. But it is none the less true that one must perceive truth so that there is a 'hearing'. 'Faith comes by hearing, and hearing by the word of God' (Rom. 10:17). Emotional stories, warnings, anecdotes or whatever cannot replace the knowledge of what grace is, what man is, who God is, who Jesus is and what saving faith is. The Holy Spirit applies truth.

I know enough about abuses of the public seeking of the Lord to turn me right off anything that resembles what I am upholding in this book. But it would be wrong to react emotionally to what is no doubt emotionalism.

This is why I have endeavoured to build my case on scripture and why I have sought to put forward a practice that honours Christ, safeguards theological integrity, allows people to respond to what they have heard and, should God be willing (blessed thought), allow Him to work in the hearts of people in an extraordinary manner.

6

A MATTER OF COURAGE

'How long will you waver between two opinions? If the Lord is God, follow him; but if Baal is God, follow him' (I Kings 18:21, NIV).

One of the grandest displays of courage to be found in all Holy Writ is the above statement of Elijah before the priests of Baal. The matter of putting oneself on the line before a godless generation characterised not only Elijah but every single one of the great men of faith in Hebrews 11. Every man that God has ever used has been one who responded to the call to come out of hiding and stand up and be counted.

Coming out of hiding takes courage. Standing up to be counted takes courage. The Christian faith is designed in part to receive cowards and make them into people of courage. Someone has defined the coward as 'a man in whom the instinct of self-preservation acts normally'.

A proof that one is really saved is that one has the courage to confess with one's mouth what one believes in one's heart. Courage is linked to saving faith in a very definite sense. Saving faith is trusting Jesus Christ alone. The proof that saving faith has emerged in the heart is that it will issue in an open, audible and visible confession.

In Jesus' day the Jews decided that 'if any man did confess that he (Jesus) was Christ, he should be put out of the synagogue' (John 9:22). 'Nevertheless among the chief rulers also many believed on him; but because of the Pharisees they did not confess him, lest they should be put out of the synagogue' (John 12:42). There were those who knew that Jesus raised Lazarus from the dead but were afraid to confess Him as Lord (John 11:46). Those who guarded the tomb of Jesus knew that Jesus was truly raised from the dead but accepted bribes not to confess this (Matt. 28:11-15). When the man who was lame from birth was instantaneously healed at the age of forty through the power of Jesus, there were those who accepted this but only wanted to persecute Jesus' disciples (Acts 4:14-16).

Does it follow that those who do not go forward in a public meeting cannot be saved? No. But they must none the less come out of hiding – sooner or later. Nicodemus came to Jesus 'by night' (John 3:2) because he wanted to converse with Jesus in hiding and, if possible, believe in hiding. There is every reason to suspect that Nicodemus *did* believe what Jesus said in John 3. The proof that Nicodemus believed *savingly*, however, is that he eventually came out of hiding, and did so in the most magnificent and self-effacing manner. After Jesus *died*, this man went openly with Joseph of Arimathea to anoint the body of Jesus. That took not only courage but faith that Jesus would be raised from the dead! For had not Jesus come out of the tomb on the third day, Nicodemus would have been the greatest fool that ever lived. But he believed in his heart. And went public with his faith.

The thief on the cross did not have the opportunity to walk down the aisle at a Billy Graham crusade but he none the less confessed Christ openly. Jesus was crucified between two criminals. On one side there was the criminal who hurled insults at Jesus: 'Aren't you the Christ? Save yourself and us!' But the other criminal rebuked him and acknowledged the righteousness of Jesus: 'We are punished justly, for we are getting what our deeds deserve. But this man has done nothing wrong.' Then this man turned to Jesus, before his fellow criminal with the crowd watching and said, 'Jesus, remember me when you come into your kingdom'. Jesus answered him, 'I tell you the truth, today you will be with me in paradise' (Luke 23:39-43, NIV). We shall meet this man in heaven.

It is not courage that saves. It is faith. But an element of courage is an ingredient in saving faith. Paul said that 'it is with your mouth that you confess and are saved' (Rom. 10:10, NIV). Why 'mouth'? So that you can be seen and heard. Who must see and hear? I should think at least two or more persons. I have often said from the pulpit before I commenced the public pledge in Westminster Chapel, 'Tell at least one other person if you have believed.' To be bibilical I should have said, tell at least *two* other persons. For Jesus said, 'In the mouth of two or three witnesses every word may be established' (Matt. 18:16). This also conformed to the Mosaic law (cf. Deut. 19:15).

Even a legal marriage has two witnesses. But that is mere legality. What is lovelier than a wedding in which many people are present to see and hear the exchanging of vows? In either case the couple are truly married. But how much more glorious when it is a marriage to which many bear witness!

So also with confessing Jesus as Lord and Saviour. Yes, you can get away with it by telling a small number. But how much greater is the witness when dozens or hundreds watch rather than merely two or three. This principle can be seen in the story of the 'sinner woman' that fell down before Jesus to wash His feet with her tears. Jesus turned to the offended Pharisee and said, 'I tell you, her many sins have been forgiven – for she loved much. But he who has been forgiven little loves little' (Luke 7:47, NIV). The one who has not sinned so notoriously as others is none the less forgiven – saved. But the one who has been forgiven much is often affected with a greater sense of gratitude. Thus the one who confesses Christ as Lord to meet the minimum requirement will be as much forgiven and assured of salvation as anybody else, but there is a certain joy with which the Christian life is launched when the confession is before many. What is more, it takes a lot more courage.

It will not take one whit of courage to confess Christ on the Last Day. And yet everybody will be doing it. Everyone. Every knee shall bow and every tongue shall confess – what? They will confess that 'Jesus is Lord'

(Phil. 2:11) – the exact confession that saves. But on the Last Day the difference will be infinite. Confessing Jesus now means salvation, doing it then – under constraint and without any faith whatsoever – will mean damnation. Sooner or later all will confess Jesus as Lord. 'Behold, he cometh with clouds; and every eye shall see him, and they also which pierced him: and all kindreds of the earth shall wail because of him. Even so, Amen' (Rev. 1:7). Neither faith nor courage will be needed then.

The public confession seals what is in the heart. It is in this sense that baptism is a seal. The public pledge temporarily takes the place of baptism and thus seals one's own commitment. For committing oneself in a public manner proves to one's own heart that one really is in earnest about following Jesus Christ.

But let me take this matter a stage further. Let us take a look at how it is often done behind the Iron Curtain. Keep in mind we are talking about courage. Earlier in this book I mentioned my friend Joseph Ton, the Romanian now living in America. I now marvel at his patience with me when he began pleading with me to call people to the front at Westminster Chapel. It was months after I began actually doing it that he told me what it was like in Romania. He kindly put his thoughts in a letter to me. It makes me so ashamed when I think how afraid I have been. For it is one thing to encourage a public pledge in a free society, quite another in Romania.

I think that one of the greatest ministries the Lord gave me was to demonstrate that under a totalitarian and brutal Communist dictatorship one could dare preach the whole counsel of God and speak openly his mind ... and survive! Now, it is true that I myself did not believe that I would survive. I actually believed they would kill me, and I prepared myself to die. I took seriously the Word of the Lord that it was better to lose my life than not confess Him ... But God shut the mouths of the lions, and I came out of the arrests and interrogations safe and victorious. *It was at that point* that I felt that my preaching of the gospel should include a challenge to confess Christ publicly as one's Saviour and Lord. I could not accept any more 'secret Christians'.

Joseph Ton further pointed out that 'in a Communist country, when one becomes a Christian and that fact becomes known, that person's job is in jeopardy'. The result may mean a 'demotion at the lowest possible level' or 'even the loss of job'. Moreover, 'all kinds of other harassments are likely'. Obviously the temptation to 'keep it secret' is very strong indeed. Then Joseph added:

You see, a challenge to stand up for Christ in that situation doesn't meet only with 'theological objections' as you have them in England. It may affect drastically the social status, the earnings, and the whole future of a whole family... [therefore] a decision made public, with all the risks involved, goes to the deepest depths of one's being... [it] made the decision to accept Christ as a total act, involving the whole being.

Always present in the services in Joseph's former church in Romania were secret policemen who were taking notes and the names of anybody who confessed Christ openly. Those who therefore made their public profession knew they were being watched. Those who accepted Christ openly in the services were later baptised. But what interested Joseph particularly was this. The real joy to the believer came not so much at the baptism – which was planned in advance – but at the moment he first stood up to be counted! It was at the moment that believers accepted Christ that 'bonds were broken' and 'fears were gone, and the joy of salvation was unspeakable. They still had to face the consequences of their decision and testimony, but the great act was done, and it was now known, and we very rarely saw a going back from it!'

Joseph added that he himself 'came to this practice through a long battle with fear and with the cowardly desire to keep a low profile', but that once he started it, the result was one of 'great liberation... I believe I was led into this practice by the Holy Spirit'.

Last year the Rev. Robert Ferguson, pastor in Kaiserslautern, West Germany, was invited to preach in Russia. At a Baptist church in Leningrad he preached to a packed church. When he finished his sermon, the pastor of the church (who was interpreting) quietly said to Mr Ferguson, 'Now give the invitation'. 'What do you mean?', Mr Ferguson asked. 'Don't you give an invitation for people to accept Christ in your church?' the pastor asked. 'Yes, but I didn't think I could do it here,' replied Mr Ferguson quite innocently. 'Go on,' the Russian pastor whispered. 'What do I do?' Mr Ferguson continued. 'Just as you do it in your own church.' Quite staggered by this unexpected conversation before over a thousand people, Mr Ferguson turned to the congregation and invited people to confess Christ openly. There was a microphone at ground level to which six different people, of all ages, came *to pray out loud* to receive Christ. Every person present *saw* it and *heard* it.

The senior minister of the Baptist church in Moscow explained to me the manner in which people accept Christ in his own church. I met the Rev. Michael Zhidkov in February 1984 when he was invited to address the International Congress on Revival in Salzburg, Austria. As we sat at dinner together, he expressed interest that I now call people forward in Westminster Chapel. He himself attended the Chapel in the 1950s when he was a student at Spurgeon's College, London. I looked at him and said, 'But surely you don't call people forward in your church?' 'Oh yes, we do,' he replied.

The way they do it in Moscow is this. When Mr Zhidkov makes his appeal, he asks for people to come to the front. 'Even the aisles are packed,' he pointed out, 'but you watch for someone trying to squeeze through the people. It's interesting to watch the movement in the aisles as people are trying to get through.' As in the church in Leningrad, microphones are stationed at ground level just beneath the pulpit. Those who come forward walk over to the microphone and *pray out loud* to receive Jesus Christ. It is open and audible to no fewer than 3,000 people. As for the person being marked Mr Zhidkov pointed out that in many cases becoming a Christian has helped the people concerned because they are 'better at their job' than previously, being more conscientious. Thus the testimony to the Christian faith can have even an ameliorating social effect. But what courage is required for people to come out of hiding in the Soviet Union.

When I consider these examples taken from Romania and Russia, then think of the minimal stigma there is in confessing Christ in the West, it seems to me to be a very small thing to ask people to do.

And yet it still takes courage. Anywhere.

The standard objection by some to all this is, 'I witness by my life'. One need not confess openly, talk to people about Christ or walk out to the front. A lot of good Jonah would have done had he entered Nineveh to witness by his life! We are commanded to confess, to witness – openly. I love Arthur Blessitt's story about the man who had 'witnessed by his life' for fifteen years. Finally one day a person on the job said to this man, 'You know, there is something different about you.' The man smiled and thought to himself how good it was to realise that after all those years somebody had noticed that he was a Christian by his godly life! 'Tell me,' continued the inquirer, 'are you a vegetarian?'

Jesus said, 'A city that is set on an hill cannot be hid' (Matt. 5:14). Being born again means that we are a new creation. 'The old has gone, the new has come!' (2 Cor. 5:17, NIV). An evidence that we have been changed is that we *will* come out of hiding. We thereby defy the old instinct of self-preservation.

Sir Wilfred Grenfell once said, 'It is courage the world needs, not infallibility... courage is always the surest wisdom.' The Apostle Paul said, 'if any man among you seemeth to be wise in this world, let him become a fool, that he may be wise' (I Cor. 3:18).

Elijah must have felt like a fool for a while. But he was

vindicated. The person who extricates himself from the
god of Baal will feel like a fool. But he will be vindicated.
The person who stands up to be counted often feels like a
fool. But he honours God in doing so and God is certain to
honour that man who honours him. 'Those who honour
me I will honour' (I Sam. 2:30, NIV).

Since I wrote the above, which I had intended to conclude
the present chapter, there came to my attention an
illustration of courage which ought to be included here.

On 22nd March 1984 Arthur Blessitt was a guest in the
home of the Marquess and Marchioness of Reading. Lord
and Lady Reading invited ninety-three guests of mixed
backgrounds from the Gloucestershire area to meet and
listen to Arthur. Seated in their drawing-room, the crowd
listened attentively to Arthur for an hour and fifteen
minutes as he spoke on the last words of Jesus from
Matthew 28:20, 'I am with you always'. He focused on the
'presence of Christ' – that Jesus is *alive* today and that He
is *real*.

At the close of his talk, Arthur felt led to invite people to
receive Christ openly. But he admitted that there was 'a
subtle pressure not to give an open call to stand up in a
setting like that with everyone's head up and eyes open'.
He did not want to offend any of the immaculately dressed
guests some of whom came from the highest professions in
the country, one or two of whom were from the House of
Lords. 'Racing through my mind was the thought to give
an invitation that would not be so absolutely obvious,'
Arthur admitted. He later said to me, 'As I stood there, I
thought of you and what you faced when you decided to
give the invitation at Westminster Chapel. In this
companionship with you I felt in a sense a little bit of what
you faced. Then I knew the Lord was saying, "Have them
stand up in front of everyone. These people must come out
in the open, it cannot be a secret call." And then I
announced it. I said, "Those who really want to receive
Jesus Christ I am going to have stand up after I pray. I will
only ask you one time." And then I prayed.'

But that is not all. 'While I was praying I felt that the Lord burdened me to lie down on the floor face down,' Arthur said. 'If you will lie down, they will stand up,' the Lord seemed to say to Arthur. 'But I found myself arguing with the Lord,' he later said. 'Here I am in my blue jeans. I don't have a suit. I'm going to ask these people to stand up openly for Jesus and the Lord wants me to lie down on the floor. Isn't there one fine cord of dignity left? Or do I have to lose it all?' But Arthur acquiesced. 'I said, "O.K., Jesus." I lay down on the floor of the drawing-room of Lord Reading, face down, flat out.'

Graham Lacey, Arthur's close friend and also a guest on this occasion, said to himself, 'This is going to be a disaster. Arthur has gone too far this time.'

Arthur then got up. He asked that everybody look up. He then continued. 'I'm going to ask you to make this commitment with every head up and every eye seeing who is committing his life to Jesus. I don't see any shame in confessing Jesus Christ. You drive down the streets with the name of your cars displayed – Volvo, Rolls Royce. You have a British passport. You are identified. Some of you have the name Lord so and so. One should not be ashamed to be identified with the Lord Jesus Christ. In the name of Jesus, stand up.'

Lord Reading said to me, 'He shook us rigid.'

Eleven people stood up. Arthur then asked that the eleven people make their way into a room off to the side. There Arthur joined them and led them in a further prayer, although he had already asked them to pray out loud while they were still standing.

When the eleven with Arthur finished their time together, to Arthur's surprise nobody in the drawing-room left. Instead they began queuing up to talk further with Arthur. One after another apologised that they did not stand, feeling ashamed.

One man walked over to Graham Lacey and said, 'I've sinned tonight.' 'What's the matter, what have you done?' Graham asked. 'I have sinned gravely tonight. I didn't stand. But I did pray the prayer and towards the end I did

say it out loud. Do you think that will do?' Graham
assured him that God accepted him.

Lord Reading was happy to give permission to tell the
above, if only that it 'might encourage other people to
open their homes' for similar occasions. He also
emphasised that the eleven people are being followed up
and encouraged to become involved in church and regular
Bible study.

7

SOME CLARIFYING QUESTIONS

Readers of *Tithing* will recall that I concluded that book with a series of questions and answers. I feel that I must anticipate every question that might come up on this issue of the public pledge, some of which still remain unanswered. My fear in doing this sort of thing in the other book was that I would still leave out some good questions and, sure enough, I have received a number of excellent questions I simply had not thought of. I know this is likely again, but I shall answer every question that either has been put to me or which I myself have anticipated.

These questions have to do with further objections to my general thesis and also those that relate to the more practical level.

1. *On the day of Pentecost Peter's hearers put the question 'What shall we do?' before he exhorted with 'many other words'. Surely we should not make an appeal or seek to lead people to close with Christ until they have initiated the whole matter.* This is the common pattern in a time of undoubted revival. We saw this in the example of Eleazar Wheelock in 1741. But I think it is sheer folly to sit still and do nothing simply because we are in a non-revival era. My concept of the public pledge keeps alive the invitation to confess Christ openly without manipulating people. It also allows room for the Holy Spirit to work in a manifest manner should He will to do it. It may also be pointed out

that the mourner's bench was constructed in the early camp meetings in America because people were *hoping* there would be seekers. And look what happened! In the very anticipation that people might inquire to seek the Lord in a public manner, the Spirit of God came down in extraordinary power. That God would come down in power like that on a gathering which erected a mourner's bench suggests that God did not disapprove of such activity. In this connection Joseph Ton once said to me, 'God never honours something He disagrees with.' I would not be too surprised if those who are afraid to move in the direction of confronting men to receive and confess Christ *now* will, at the end of the day, see little fruit from their labours.

2. *Will the public pledge increase the number of the elect?* No. Of course not. Neither does revival. But in the time of blessing there is always the appearance of conversions which, humanly speaking, might not otherwise have taken place. Revival does not increase the number of God's elect but it none the less results in so many conversions that one is *tempted* to say that people are being saved that otherwise would have perished. Whether God sends revival or honours the public pledge in the meantime, one can only say with Paul, 'O the depth of the riches both of the wisdom and knowledge of God! how unsearchable are his judgments, and his ways past finding out!' (Rom. 11:33).

3. *Is there not a danger of people coming out to the front under sheer emotional pressure?* Yes. I have sought to guard against precisely this in the present book. If a person comes forward under emotional pressure, it does not follow, however, that no good can come from it. The evil that may follow of course is when such a person thinks he is saved simply because he walked out to the front. This is where counsellors come into the picture. The person who walked forward under emotional pressure needs to be told precisely what salvation is. If that person who came forward under pressure is subsequently shown that no

conversion has taken place, even good can come of it – not to mention the fact that valuable literature can be placed in his hands. Moreover the follow-up can eventually issue in true conversion which, humanly speaking, might not have happened had the person not come out to the front. There is no proof that all who make professions even in a time of true revival are truly converted, neither can one be sure that the band waggon effect was entirely missing. Furthermore, there is no scheme or system – or the practice of doing nothing – which guarantees that all who make professions, whatever the conditions, are absolutely saved. Even those who refuse to give appeals must deal with the unregenerate person who took the initiative and who may end up joining the Church.

4. *What about people who are sorry 'the day after' they walked out to the front?* I would have thought that this reaction could even be more likely with the one who really was converted. If the counterfeit 'got through' the process of walking forward and being counselled, he may have little regret over what he did. He will also know in his heart whether he is playing a game. I do not think that there are a great many people who truly regard themselves as *born again* who also walked to the front hypocritically. A person like that is usually not deceived by the system of walking out to the front but self-deceived because he did not come clean with himself. As for the one who was totally sincere and who prayed to receive Christ from his heart, it is not surprising that the devil will give him a real battle the next day.

5. *What about children? Should children be encouraged to go out to the front?* In my view they should not be discouraged if it is what they truly, voluntarily and earnestly want to do. Arthur Blessitt was seven years old when he cried all the way home in the back seat of his parents' car when they would not let him walk forward in a tent meeting in Louisiana. Finally they turned around, went back to the place where the meeting had been going

on, discovered that the evangelist was still there, then asked him to come to the car and pray with their son. The evangelist did. Arthur knew he was saved. He went forward the next night. I know that this is a delicate matter and I am trying to be as candid as possible. But I would have thought that there is more danger to the child's future spiritual progress should he or she be discouraged from walking forward if he so desires. If anyone goes forward prematurely, time will reveal such; what is more, the person himself will eventually come to terms with the truth.

The man I referred to in a previous chapter who walked forward because he knew he would get a silver dollar, knew in his heart that he was *not* saved that way. The man is an evangelist today. I would add my own view that in a time of true revival one can expect an *avalanche* of activity among the very young. I would not aim for children in my call for a public pledge, neither would I discourage them – nor be discouraged should a child be the only one to come out to the front.

6. *How does the public pledge in the sermon change the structure of the service as a whole?* Very little. One usually has a closing hymn after the sermon anyway; why not let this time be used in a wider manner than congregational singing? In other words, the public pledge adds very little time to the service itself. If the preacher has made it clear that he is going to invite people to make a public pledge to the honour of Jesus Christ and explains what he means by it, no more need be done than sing the hymn. When one or more walk to the front, I usually walk down from the pulpit to meet them, then turn them over to a counsellor, who takes them back to a private room. When the hymn is over, I might make a comment or two by way of expressing joy over the one who came out; then I give the benediction.

7. *When in the sermon should one insert the call for the public pledge?* Billy Graham often begins his sermon with the challenge that all who have never received Christ will

be given an opportunity to do so before the evening is over. He explains what they will have the opportunity to do, preaches his sermon, then brings the matter of closing with Christ home. I think this is ideal.

I myself do not always make it clear at the beginning of each sermon. By now most who come to my evening services expect it at the end. What I always try to do, however, is to anticipate the one who has not heard of such an opportunity, then make it as clear as I know how to do. As I said earlier, I often pray a prayer which I ask them to repeat in their heart. This I do at the very end of my sermon. Then I say, 'If you prayed that prayer and are not ashamed of it, share it with us.'

Or I might simply summarise how to be saved: 'Do you recognise that you are lost? That you are a sinner? Do you acknowledge that you cannot save yourself? Do you confess that your only hope is in the blood which Jesus shed on the cross? Do you confess that Jesus is the Son of God – that He is God in the flesh? Are you prepared to commit your life to Him on this very night?' Then I will ask them to stand up and be counted.

I then lead the congregation in prayer. I always point out that I am going to pray before we begin the final hymn; otherwise people will begin reaching for their hymnals and the rustling of the pages can be distracting. I always say, 'After we pray, we will sing a final hymn.' As I said earlier, I am still trying to improve on my own way of doing it. However one acts, one must feel comfortable.

8. *Even though the public pledge might be different from that of some high-pressure evangelists, is there not a danger in being identified in some sense with the phonies and charlatans?* One must be willing to make oneself of no reputation, even letting people think what they will when one does what appears to resonate with the undesirable. What is certain is this: the practice of public confession or seeking the Lord has a respectable history; it was born in revival. When Pharaoh's magicians matched Aaron's practice of throwing down his rod and seeing it turn into a

serpent, did Aaron abandon the practice? No. He threw down his rod again and watched his rod swallow up those of the counterfeit. Merely because the counterfeit practice comes in and gives a valid practice a bad reputation is not a good enough reason to abandon it and leave it to the abusers.

9. *Who should be included when inviting people to respond publicly? How far do you go in allowing people to come forward to profess everything from faith in Christ to joining a church?* My idea of public pledge is intended to be non-provincial, non-parochial. Surely the call to confess Christ openly should transcend culture and minor theological differences? It is the public pledge I recommend, not the embellishments that some feel strongly about. The public pledge is confessing Christ openly but also allowing the earnest seeker to express himself by walking out to the front. That alone is what I am pressing home. I have also stated that there is a place for the back-slider renewing his vows in a public manner, especially if it is known that a certain person has not been living for the Lord. His return to the fold can bring great encouragement to the church. Beyond that I would not want to get too involved. What churches want to do in various parts of the world is up to them. When I was a Southern Baptist pastor I too invited people to come forward to request church membership because that was the custom.

10. *What do you mean by follow-up?* This is a cliché that is not likely to go away in connection with staying in touch with all those who commit themselves in a public manner. The need at some stage to get people's names, find out why they came out to the front, find out whether they have assurance of salvation, explain the gospel again, show the implications of the gospel for living the Christian life and what such people ought to do from now on, is essential. D. L. Moody thought that people needed to understand the 'theology of conversion'. This can happen in the follow-up. The result often is that the

people are converted as a consequence of the follow-up.

Arthur Blessitt has often said that the follow-up is more important than anything else. I have often used his own pamphlet 'The New Life' when dealing with the person who I thought had been truly converted. Showing what has taken place in the heart of the new believer, the outline is: (1) Jesus has come to live within your heart. (2) Your sins are forgiven. (3) You are saved. (4) You have received eternal life. (5) You are now a child of God. (6) The Holy Spirit abides within you. (7) You have become a new person. (8) Your relationship with other people has changed. The next part of the pamphlet 'The New Life' asks 'What to do now?' (1) Pray daily. (2) Read the Bible daily. (3) Witness for Christ daily. (4) Confess Christ openly and be baptised. (5) Attend church where the Bible is preached and Christ is honoured. (6) Keep Christ's commandments. More of course is said under these various statements, including scriptural references. It is important to ask whether or not the person has a Bible. At Westminster Chapel we give away Gideon Bibles to all new converts if they don't already have a Bible. The counsellor will take notes on a sheet which we have prepared for the potential convert. One hopes to keep in touch with the person. Relationships can develop between the counsellor and convert that can endure if the new convert lives near enough to the church to keep coming. Otherwise we would try to find a church in the area from which that person comes. We then contact a minister in that area if we believe he will show a keen interest in the new convert.

11. *What are the requirements for a counsellor?* First, that the counsellor himself knows that he is saved. Second, that he has a good grasp of the gospel and the way of salvation. Third, that he is personable and able to talk with a totally new person. Fourth, that he is sensitive to the leadership of the Holy Spirit. Fifth, that he has a good appearance, that is, dressed in a manner that is not distracting; that he/she looks neat, etc. I tend to have a lady talk with another lady

and a man with another man, although an older lady can talk with a younger man with no temptations to distraction, etc.

12. *What should a counsellor say to the person who has walked out to the front?* Generally speaking, I would suggest the following. He/she should first introduce himself and say how glad he is that this person has walked forward. It is sometimes then good to ask, 'Do you know why you have come forward?' No matter what the answer is, in most cases, one cannot do better than to proceed with the two famous questions used in Evangelism Explosion. 'Do you know for certain that if you were to die tonight you would go to heaven?' Regardless of the answer I would then proceed to the second question, 'If you were to die and found yourself standing before God and He were to say to you, "Why should I let you into my heaven?" what would you say?' This brings a person face to face with the ground of salvation and the ground of assurance. What is needed from that point on, should the answer to the second question betray a hope in one's good works, etc., is a straightforward presentation of the gospel. A counsellor should be able to do this. Should the answer reveal that the person has a clear hope of salvation I recommend the aforementioned pamphlet 'The New Life'.

13. *If a minister or evangelist is not sure whether he should present the public pledge in his congregation, should he none the less give it a try for a month or two?* No. Until the minister is persuaded in his heart that it is right, he will waver indefinitely. One must be committed to this, whether or not it works. If one tries it once and a person goes forward, does this make it right? Surely not. Conversely, if one calls for people to commit themselves publicly and nobody comes, does this make it wrong? Hardly. One must 'go for broke', putting oneself on the line from now until Jesus comes if one is going to be blessed in this practice. But when you are persuaded in your heart, you will have peace. Even if you feel like a fool.

14. *If nobody comes forward, can this not spoil a good sermon?* In some ways, yes, for both the minister and the people. Before I began calling people forward in Westminster I needed two things, generally speaking, to give me a good feeling at the end of the day: to have preached well and a good congregation. Now there is a third – a good response when I present the public pledge. When I have preached unusually well (according to my wife) but nobody has come forward I am vulnerable to underestimating the good that may have come during the day. I am getting over this, if only because when I have preached poorly (according to my wife) the response is sometimes almost extraordinary! 'We have this treasure in earthen vessels, that the excellency of the power may be of God, and not of us' (2 Cor. 4:7). It is also true that a disappointing response to the public pledge can disquiet the congregation. One must simply get over this and believe one is right in oneself whether or not people respond. After all, our peace and joy must ultimately come from God. When one has settled this matter in one's heart, one is much less vulnerable to feeling downcast if nobody responds to the public call to commitment.

15. *What about having counsellors walk forward in order to encourage others to follow?* I am against this. This truly borders on the wholly psychological approach and I would never allow it under my own preaching. It is true, however, that those who do go forward unpretentiously will encourage others. This is another matter. But to let Christians do this with the express purpose of making it easy for others to follow is a vote of 'no confidence' in the Holy Spirit.

16. *But is not the 'power of suggestion' the same, whether or not the counsellor triggers the response or the earnest person?* This is possibly true. But what I equally believe is this: when a person does walk out to the front under the power of the Spirit, there is sometimes a releasing of the Spirit in the congregation that can be felt most

powerfully. This to me is not a fleshly power of suggestion but a way in which the Spirit may choose to move. I have seen it happen many times. The same Holy Spirit who can be quenched (I Thess. 5:19) will often move most powerfully once a person 'breaks the ice'. One reason I know this is true is because in many cases the second or third person who went forward had not been aware that anybody else had moved out previously. Moreover, the one who does go out first often shames the person who is tottering on the fence. In any case, the Spirit often works in this manner and it should not be regarded as fleshly. It can be that of course, but it is often the power of God at work. When God wills to work in this way the atmosphere is heavenly.

17. *But surely this whole approach to things is to encourage the kind of counterfeit conversion foretold by Jesus in the parable of the sower (Matt. 13:3–23)?* Possibly. But what it also does is to show the validity of the parable of the sower in a way which is scarcely seen in today's Christianity. If one were to inspect some churches one would think there never was a need for the parable of the sower – buildings filled with aged saints and little else. The parable of the sower was envisaged by Jesus as the *normal situation.* An atmosphere in which *all kinds* of things are happening is what ought to be normal. But so many are afraid to do anything that will let in any possibility of the counterfeit. The parable of the sower is dignified by a church that is having to cope with every conceivable response to the gospel. Evangelist Vance Havner said, 'Some are so afraid to get out on a limb they never get up the tree.' If it is ever said of your church, 'More counterfeit Christians profess faith there than any place in our area', I guarantee that it will also be true that more people are *saved* in your church than anywhere else in the area. A ministry or church that protects itself in such a manner that renders the parable of the sower redundant will be a dead church. The cynics love to point out those who 'never last'. But those who *do* last, being converted in

an atmosphere which dignifies the parable of the sower, will probably outnumber the *total* professions (true and false) of that church which feverishly protects itself from seed sown by the 'way side'. Unless there is an indiscriminate, lavish and enthusiastic sowing of seed there will be little happening in that church, not to mention the rarity of the true conversion.

Some people see the parable of the sower as a warning lest we have anything happening but what springs from 'good ground'. I see the parable of the sower as a pattern of what the ideal ministry can expect when one answers the call to evangelise indiscriminately. Anybody who is trying to protect the Church from conditions that resemble the parable of the sower will be like the man who hid his talent in the ground because he did not want to rob God of any glory (cf. Matt. 25:24ff). The result will be an abnormal situation as far as what Jesus envisaged is concerned.

18. *What advice is there for the person who once went forward in a public meeting but since has fallen away?* Such a person should at once go where he can hear the gospel of Jesus Christ. He should ask God for mercy. If there comes within his heart a real conviction that Jesus is Lord, he should be encouraged. 'No man can say that Jesus is the Lord but by the Holy Ghost' (I Cor. 12:3). If he believes in his heart that God raised Jesus from the dead, he ought to confess this with his mouth – even if he has done it before. If it was a premature confession the previous time, this should not discourage the person (or anybody else) from hoping that it is real this time.

I would like to relate a story that has relevance here. Within a few weeks of our commencement of the public call to commitment at Westminster, alongside our Pilot Light work in the streets, there were those in the congregation who were critical because of (1) the 'type of person' that was being converted and (2) the fact that so many of those converted were seldom seen in the Chapel because they did not live close enough to come very often. One person who had been a supporter of my ministry warned me that some of the older members in the church were against what we were doing – both on Sunday evenings (public pledge) and Saturday mornings (Pilot Lights). One Saturday morning during those hard days my wife and I joined hands in prayer and asked God to bring someone to us from the immediate area of the Chapel. Within two hours of that prayer a lady passed by the steps of the Chapel. I spoke to her, gave her a tract and tried to persuade her to talk with me a few minutes about the Lord. She refused, then paused long enough for me to pray for her. I did not know if I would ever see her again. Two weeks later after the Sunday evening service the same lady came to see me in the vestry. With tears rolling down her face she commented on a young person who went forward in the service. She then began to sob her heart out. 'When I was a teenager I did that once,' she said. 'Is there any hope for me now?' I went over the gospel with her in detail and led her to the Lord in my vestry. The following Sunday night she chose to walk forward again. Six months later I baptised her. Within a year after her conversion she became a member of Westminster Chapel. She lived a hundred yards from the Chapel.

19. *What advice is there for the person who is not sure of his salvation because he has not gone forward publicly, even though he has had the opportunity?* I would first ask that person what his hope was with regard to going to heaven, that is, I would ask the second question as above in question twelve. If the answer showed that the person was trusting Jesus Christ alone for salvation I would assure him that he was saved. If this did not satisfy him, obviously he could always walk out to the front if this would give him some release. Baptism might come into the picture, not to mention how much he witnessed for Christ. But I would never want anybody to think that the public pledge is the only way a person can have assurance of salvation.

20. *To what extent does enthusiasm and emotionalism*

come into the picture when one is faced with the public call to commitment? Most certainly one's emotions are involved. The appeal should be to the mind, heart and will – in that order. Clive Calver has called the message of the gospel 'a call to crisis'. This immediately gives a person pause, thus affecting the emotions. Enthusiasm can also play a part, especially if the evangelist or preacher is gifted with eloquence or the ability to tell anecdotes. If the Holy Spirit is at work I do not see how He would by-pass man's affective nature; emotions do come into play, whether or not a public pledge is an option.

I would also say that if the emotions *only* are affected and if one is merely enthusiastic because of the personality of the evangelist, then the person obviously has not been converted by the Holy Spirit. And yet it is also possible that one can be saved 'unemotionally', that is, when the display of emotionalism is totally absent. Clive Calver adds that the commitment therefore 'does not need to be emotional'. But by that he means a manifest display of emotionalism, the sort of thing which D. L. Moody feared. But even when emotionalism is not apparent, I cannot conceive of one being converted and not being touched emotionally in some way. It is simply that not all show their emotions.

21. *What about the minister or evangelist getting the congregation to sing extra verses of the final hymn in order to persuade more people to walk forward?* I am against it. As I said in a previous chapter, I felt led to sing the first verse of our final hymn again on one occasion. I am sure that I was then led by the Spirit. I would not hesitate to do this in Westminster if I truly felt the Spirit was present in power. But to beg and plead with people to walk forward and then keep singing more verses is in my view an abuse of all that I am putting forward in this book. Doing this sort of thing smacks of manipulation rather than the work of the Spirit.

22. *What advice is there for the layman whose minister*

will not call people forward to confess Christ publicly?
Support him totally. Love him and respect his reasons for
the procedure he feels most comfortable with. He may feel
differently six months or two years from now, but should
any layman put the slightest pressure on his vicar or
minister, it would almost always betray impatience on the
part of the layman – which grieves the Holy Spirit. 'Let
patience have her perfect work' (Jas. 1:4). If God is truly
dealing with any man along these lines, it is best to let that
dialogue go on between the minister and God alone. The
same God who has been leading your minister or vicar up
to now will continue to direct. In my own case, God has
been abundantly patient with me – so much so that I
blush. I could never nudge the arm of God's providence
with the next man and feel good about it. God's dealings
with me require me to follow Job: 'I will lay mine hand
upon my mouth' (Job 40:4).

23.　*What advice is there for those who have a lingering
concern over the type of people who will walk out to the
front?* I must say candidly that until one reaches the place
where one wants the same kind of people that flocked to
Jesus, blessing will be postponed in that church. The error
of the Christians James addressed was that they were
discriminating in their evangelistic outreach. They
wanted to reach a certain 'class'. They treated the poor
man with contempt and the rich man with dignity. Did it
work? No, it did not. The rich did not respect these
Christians (Jas. 2:6–7). Furthermore you can mark it down
that these Christians didn't reach the poor. Aim for the
rich and you will miss the poor and scare away the rich.
Aim for the poor and you will reach *everybody*. The public
pledge opens the floodgates so that all kinds will flock to
the front. If you don't want that, I think you should
examine whether or not you really want a New Testament
church at all.

24.　*Surely the public call to commitment will work in a
place like Westminster Chapel but nowhere else?* Non-

sense. Gospel halls all over Britain have been doing this for years. So have the Salvation Army, Methodists and Baptists. I really think it is mostly two things that keep us from this practice: fear and pride. We must bear the cross, wear a stigma, make ourselves of no reputation and go after the lost of this world with unrestrained zeal. I could give you every reason why Westminster Chapel is the last place this practice should work.

Arthur Blessitt says that nearly everywhere he goes the pastor or church leader will usually say of their particular area, 'Ours is the hardest place of all.'

Conclusion

'Which evangelist shall we invite to Britain after Billy Graham and Luis Palau?' I am sorry to have to say it, but this question has been asked again and again.

What a pity. Surely evangelism is the work of the church – the local church. But if men like Billy Graham and Luis Palau can inspire us to keep up what they have started, this makes their coming more worthwhile than if we were just looking at the numbers that were converted through 'Mission to London' and 'Mission England'.

One of these days Dr Billy Graham will make his last visit to Great Britain. It has been reported that some 200,000 have been converted so far over here through his ministry alone. But what would be his greater legacy, surely, is that the Church takes the need for mass evangelism completely away . . . by doing what it ought to be doing all the time.

Appendix I

Theological glossary

Arminianism. Jacobus Arminius, latinised name for Jacob Haemensz (c. 1559-1609), was a Dutch theologian who reacted against the doctrine of predestination as it was taught in his day. Arminius studied under Theodore Beza in Geneva. After he died, his ideas were kept alive by his followers, known as the Remonstrants. In 1610 the Remonstrants put forward five tenets: (1) God has designated Jesus Christ as the Redeemer of men and decreed to save all who believe on Him; (2) Christ died for all but only believers enjoy forgiveness of sins; (3) man must be regenerated by the Spirit; (4) grace is 'not irresistible'; and (5) perseverance is granted 'through the assistance of the grace of the Holy Spirit', but whether one can fall away from 'life in Christ' is left open. In a word: God predestines those who believe. This became known as Arminianism.

Calvinism. John Calvin (1509-64) taught that Christ died indiscriminately for all men but that 'all that He has suffered and done for the salvation of the human race remains useless and of no value for us' until one believes. The power to believe is wholly the gift of God and it is only bestowed upon those God has chosen by His secret decree. Calvin called predestination 'God's eternal decree, by which he compacted with himself what he willed to become of each man'. To Calvin the doctrine of election was the hidden explanation why some believe. In a word: those who believe were predestined by God to do so.

High Calvinism. In 1619–20 the international Synod of Dordrecht (Dort) condemned Arminianism and adopted a position which became known as Calvinism, or reformed theology. Calvin's successor in Geneva, Theodore Beza, revived the scholastic teaching of a limited atonement and this view was linked to Calvin's name. The Canons of Dort are: (1) that God's eternal decree of predestination is the cause of election and reprobation [non-election], and that this decree is not based upon foreseen faith; (2) that Christ died for the elect only [limited atonement]; (3) and (4) that men by nature are unable to seek God apart from the Spirit and that grace is irresistible; and (5) the elect will surely persevere in faith to the end. This eventually was systematised into the popular acrostic TULIP: total depravity, unconditional election, limited atonement, irresistible grace, perseverance of the saints. Although some may wish to dispute this, because the teaching of limited atonement is missing in Calvin's actual writings, I am compelled to regard traditional reformed theology as 'high Calvinism'. (For further study see my *Calvin and English Calvinism to 1649*, Oxford University Press, 1979).

Hyper-Calvinism. This is a spirit that militates against evangelism and the free offer of the gospel. It has its roots in high Calvinism but goes beyond it. Many high Calvinists would still hold to the free offer of the gospel – that you should offer the gospel to everyone even though Christ did not die for everyone. Hyper-Calvinism holds that one must not say 'Christ died for you' lest one should not be telling the truth. The most that the hyper-Calvinist feels that he can do is to say 'Christ died for sinners' and leave the rest to the Holy Spirit. Hyper-Calvinism does not essentially differ from high Calvinism except in actual practice, which is why I define hyper-Calvinism as a spirit.

Pelagianism. Named after the British monk Pelagius (*fl.* 410), who taught that man took the initial and funda-mental steps towards salvation by his own efforts apart from the assistance of Divine grace. Pelagius reacted against the teachings of Augustine who, in turn, refined his own teaching of predestination by writing against Pelagius.

Conversion. The act by which a person is translated from the kingdom of darkness to light. It is being 'born again' and is never separated from faith and repentance.

Faith. Trusting Jesus Christ alone; transferring all hope in ourselves to all that Jesus did for us.

Justification. The forgiveness of sins and the imputation of Christ's righteousness to all who believe the gospel. To impute means 'to put to the credit of'

Regeneration. Being born again; the hidden work of God the Holy Spirit that lies behind repentance and faith.

Repentance. A change of mind; agreeing with God; admitting 'I was wrong'.

Sanctification. The process by which one is made holy after conversion. After the time of John Wesley the phrase 'entire sanctification' emerged, as well as the term 'sanctified wholly'. This eventually became an experience to be sought – as distinct from conversion, but only in the Holiness Movement.

Appendix II

In this appendix I summarize my case with the following twenty-two statements.

1. *It is an appeal to the whole man.* By presenting the public pledge to a congregation one appeals not to the mind only but also to the heart and the will.

2. *It goes right against the grain of the natural man.* The self-preservation instinct in man recoils at the thought of confessing the Lord openly and publicly. This is why Jesus called men publicly. It is why men are commanded to come out of hiding.

3. *It temporarily takes the place of baptism.* Baptism was the ultimate and most powerful way in which one confessed Christ in the early Church. Most certainly baptism fulfils the basic requirement of Matthew 10:32–3 and Romans 10:9–10.

4. *It dignifies the New Testament practice of not waiting to confess after one has truly believed.* On the day of Pentecost there was no committee organised to interview candidates to see how much they grasped or how earnest they were to follow the Lord. If they asked for baptism, they got it, with its considerable offence.

The public pledge is nothing like the stigma the early Church faced. But it is still an opportunity to confess Christ at the earliest possible moment. In the early Church a person went out in the open as soon as he believed. The public pledge gives one an opportunity to do that.

5. *It launches the Christian life in a very happy manner*. To the person who believed the gospel and then walked out to the front there is great joy.

6. *It presses home the urgency to confess Jesus Christ as Saviour and Lord*. I suspect that many, many people who have sat under sound gospel preaching have been largely undisturbed by it because there has been no call for immediate decision. Even if the preacher managed to say all the right things – including 'you must believe this today' – many people still don't get the point. But hearing the minister say, 'I am going to give you an opportunity to confess Jesus Christ tonight by *coming from your seat to the front*', the urgency of the matter is immediately felt.

7. *It provides an immediate contact with those with whom the Holy Spirit has been at work*. Even if those who do come forward are not saved, we now have an opportunity to keep in touch with those we would otherwise never have known about.

8. *It enables the church to know about the person most recently converted*. It is a shame when a person comes to faith but nobody finds out about it. It is partly the person's own fault, yes. But oftentimes that person does not know any better. If anyone is not told to come out of hiding he will most likely remain in hiding, as it were; he simply lacked instruction about making his faith known.

9. *It encourages people to bring their non-Christian friends to hear the gospel, lest their minister preach the gospel only to the converted week after week*. I know a number of ministers who would dearly love to preach the gospel more often, but there are rarely non-Christians present to motivate him to do so. After all, it is a bit disheartening for the minister when he prepares a gospel sermon to the lost, then faces only the saints when the time comes for him to preach it.

10. *It lets the visitor or stranger feel that he is wanted and accepted.* The very moment the public pledge is presented to the congregation, *everybody* instinctively feels it. The public pledge sends a signal to the stranger that *he matters.* When he first comes into the church he may think, 'Nobody here cares about me. Nobody in this place will notice me.'

11. *It visibly demonstrates the truth that all are accepted as they are.* The hymn 'Just as I am, without one plea' often seems too good to be true. But it is true. Jesus accepts us as we are. A person can therefore feel he may walk out to the front just as he is – without any further preparation – and be accepted in Jesus Christ.

12. *It gives people an opportunity to respond to what they have just heard.* The public pledge is an opportunity. It is a responsibility, yes. But it is essentially an opportunity to express what one feels in one's heart.

13. *It releases the Holy Spirit to work more freely.* This of course overlaps with point six above. For the urgency one feels as a consequence of the public call to commitment is the Holy Spirit's pressure. But I mean more than that here. The Holy Spirit is often quenched once the gospel service is over. Once a person has left the church building, he goes back to the routine of things and is able to shake off any troubled feeling he may have had when he was in the service. But when the public pledge is called for, the Spirit can then and there drive home all that has been understood.

14. *It provides a further witness to those who did not go forward by those who did.* Those who have the courage to stand up and be counted in this manner will not realise it at the time, but their very act of walking out to the front serves both to encourage and to shame those who ought to have done the same thing. They therefore are witnessing before *all* men – saved and unsaved – and are having an

impact on those who watch. This can be a most powerful witness indeed. One's obedience will inspire or shame others.

15. *It is a light to all the world*. A church in which the public pledge is called for will soon get a reputation. This reputation is unmistakable: here is a church that still believes in the historic gospel; here is a church that believes people need to be saved; here is a church that expects people to be saved.

16. *It provides an opportunity to see the Holy Spirit at work*. I used to go home on a Sunday night wondering whether anybody was moved by the gospel and if anybody might have been saved. So also did many people. 'I wonder if God was at work tonight?' people would ask.

17. *It is fishing for men*. All gospel preaching is this of course, but the call for a public pledge is what W. A. Criswell describes as 'drawing in the net'. When any minister has just preached the gospel to the lost, he often betrays how much he really believes it by how earnestly he calls people to believe that same gospel.

18. *It can bring life and excitement to the church*. Nothing is as electrifying to a church as the sight of someone walking out to the front in an atmosphere in which there is great conviction and power. I am sure that in many cases the people who watch are happier than the one who walks to the front. The person who walks to the front is often shaking with timidity and self-consciousness, but the people who watch are filled with joy.

19. *It can bring great encouragement to the minister*. To the minister who will go out on a limb and do what has not been generally done, there is a lot of anxiety. A lot. But the sight of seeing somebody walk out to the front probably brings greater joy to the minister than to anybody else.

20. *It goes right against Satan's chief aim.* I cannot emphasise enough the point that Satan hates indiscriminate evangelism. He will do all he can to coerce us to 'tone it down' or settle for a 'certain type'. Satan will not be pleased when a church gets excited about reaching the lost.

21. *It brings rejoicing in heaven in the presence of the angels.* When there is indiscriminate evangelism, it will keep the angels singing. I like to think of having to initiate a concert in heaven every Sunday night. 'I say unto you, there is joy in the presence of the angels of God over one sinner that repenteth' (Luke 15:10).

22. *It is honouring to God.* It is honouring to God because it is honouring to His purpose in sending His Son. The public pledge honours the gospel. It honours the blood which Jesus shed on the cross. It honours the holiness of God. It honours the sovereignty of God. It honours the justice of God. For in the gospel of Jesus Christ all of God's attributes come together.